The New Political Economy
of the Pacific

The New
Political
Economy of
the Pacific

Edited by
Bernard K. Gordon
Kenneth J. Rothwell

Ballinger Publishing Company ● Cambridge, Mass.
A Subsidiary of J.B. Lippincott Company

International Standard Book Number: 0–88410–279–3

Library of Congress Catalog Card Number: 75–4717

Printed in the United States of America

Library of Congress Cataloging in Publication Data

Main entry under title:

The new political economy of the Pacific.

  Essays which originated at a conference held at the New England Center
for Continuing Education, April, 1973.
1. Oceanica–Economic conditions–Congresses.
2. Oceanica–Foreign economic relations–Congresses.
3. Oceanica–Foreign relations–Congresses.
I. Gordon, Bernard K., 1932–   II. Rothwell, Kenneth J.
HC683.N48   330.9'9   75–4717
ISBN 0–88410–279–3

Contents

List of Tables

Preface

This collection of essays is concerned with the dramatically changing alignments—political and economic—which have taken place in the 1970s in the Pacific Basin. A new balance is being struck in this region and its cumulative consequences will carry into the 1980s. Experts have varying interpretations on how the changes will affect the world system; some of these views are captured in this volume.

These essays originated at a conference on "The New Political Economy in the Pacific" sponsored by the International Studies Council of the University of New Hampshire and held at the New England Center for Continuing Education in April 1973.* Subsequent revisions and additions were made to incorporate views generated in ensuing discussions among groups of experts drawn both from a number of academic disciplines and from research and government posts. Participants from Asia Society, Brookings Institution, U.S. State Department, Japanese Consul General, Woodrow Wilson International Center, and International Bank for Reconstruction and Development, as well as numerous universities, helped give the discussions and analyses broad perspectives.

Very recently, but beginning not much longer ago than the 1960s, there have been impressive efforts to deepen significantly American understanding of Asia, and to broaden the scope of that understanding among much wider portions of the American people than ever before. A recognition of how much needs to be done led initially to the planning of the "Pacific Basin" symposium which is reflected in the papers that make up this volume. As scholars concerned

---

*Initial planning and much of the organization of the conference were the responsibility of the editors and two colleagues: Professor Frank McCann of the History Department at the University of New Hampshire and Professor Donald Sherk of the Economics Department at Simmons College. Their assistance is warmly acknowledged.

with various aspects of America's role in world affairs, we and others at the University of New Hampshire and elsewhere were concerned to bring together a wide variety of perspectives on Pacific area relations and to place these within the framework of history as well as of contemporary economic and political relations in the area.

Because of different styles of presentation and varied institutional perspectives, depending partly upon the subject matter and partly upon the author involved, the essays contained in this volume do not strive for identity of organization, argument and documentation. Partly for that reason, each section is preceded by an introduction which identifies and develops the theme of that section and there are in addition chapters which critically review the major papers.

The divisions in this volume seek to separate basic approaches to the new political economy relations: a statement of the context of the problems; the historical emergence; the economic forces; and the evolving political strategies for national security. The joint editors of the materials presented here have received help from many quarters, official and academic, private and public, and from critical and approving commentators. Nevertheless, they share joint responsibility for the statements and selections of views presented.

Bernard K. Gordon
Kenneth J. Rothwell

Part I

The Context of Contemporary Conflict and Cooperation: An Overview

Chapter One

Introduction

*Bernard K. Gordon and
Kenneth J. Rothwell*

For generations, the Pacific has exercised a powerful, almost magnetic attraction on the interest and imagination of Westerners, and for Americans in particular the region has had the aura and appeal of the exotic and the romantic. The notions of the "inscrutable Orient" and Bali Hai bring on a sentimental smile today, but the world of Pacific Asia did indeed seem mysterious and almost unknowable in the pre-jet age, especially in that earlier era when the words "China Clipper" did not yet mean a Pan American amphibian, and certainly not a jet.

In those years, very few Westerners had had direct experience in the Pacific. We tend to forget how small were the contingents of merchants and soldiers, missionaries and occasional educators who knew the "East." This was partly because of the great disparity between the cultures, and especially the technological capabilities, of the two worlds. In military terms, for example, relatively few soldiers were required either to "conquer" or to control the various empires that were established. French Indochina is a good case in point: at the height of empire, in the late nineteenth century, there appear to have been almost as many French school teachers as there were soldiers in what is now Vietnam, Cambodia and Laos.

Another factor lies in the aims of empire that were established and sought in Asia. These were quite different from the motives that brought Spain and Portugal to the Latin American rim of the Pacific in an earlier era. For in Asia there was no parallel to the tens of thousands of *conquistadors* who came to conquer, to intermarry and to stay. With the partial exception of the missionaries, the Westerners in Asia came instead only to the main towns and cities, in small numbers, and they concerned themselves primarily with trade and commerce during the relatively short periods of their stay. To the extent that they sought political and economic "control," this generally was achieved

3

through some local middleman—a Sultan, a Chinese manager, or other local chieftain or mandarin.

For these Westerners, "home" was still the village and garden near London, Rotterdam or Boston from which they had set out, to which they would shortly return, and where most often their wives and children remained and carried out their normal lives. Even in the case of the Philippines, where the pattern of American colonization was by comparison more "enlightened" than any that had gone before, involvement of Americans was largely restricted to the U.S. Army and a small number of businessmen and teachers. One manifestation is that the Philippines, despite almost fifty years of American colonization, is still *terra incognita* to us, and most Americans have never heard of such Philippine national saints and heroes as Rizal and Aguinaldo.

Until and even after the Second World War, as a result of these patterns of indirect rule and relatively limited colonial goals, the West remained quite ignorant of the peoples and societies of the Pacific. It has been only in the past generation, despite the preceding near-century of extensive colonial contact, that intensive Western awareness and real familiarity regarding the Pacific has developed. Americans in particular, in the tens of thousands, have traveled and worked in the Pacific in the postwar era, in a development that both preceded and was independent of the Vietnam war. The explanation for this recent and much broader contact lies in a prediction that was made long ago by early visitors and occasional dreamers: that someday the Pacific would occupy center stage of human attention.

That prediction has certainly come true, for the Pacific—especially its Asian rim—has supplanted even Europe in the view of many Westerners. For some it is a market of major importance, and its role as a supplier of so many products in such volume that often it appears a threat to jobs and security is well-known. For others, Pacific Asia is a region from which to draw models and lessons for many kinds of human behavior—ranging from paths of economic development and the tactics of guerilla war to "ways" of achieving inner peace. For still others the importance of the Pacific is that it is a portion of the political globe especially marked by instability and turmoil. Seen in this light the problems of the Pacific can lead to conflicts capable of enveloping the superpowers, with potentially disastrous consequences for every individual. But for all the central point is the same: the Pacific impacts too heavily upon us today, in so many ways, any longer to be regarded as inscrutable.

The nature of our recent involvements in the Pacific has meant that Americans in particular have been exposed (often literally) to "crash courses" about the region, and that sense of urgency has been part of that process. For the concept of *threat*—both political and economic—has largely characterized the recent heightened American concern with the region, and this differs from the concept and approach with which Europeans originally encountered the area.

For them, the initial attraction and magnetism of Asia was largely one of opportunity—for political expansion, for profit, for new religious and ideological fields to conquer, and for related goals of a relatively positive nature. This historically defensive or negative nature of the American involvement may help to explain why historically there has been so little American understanding of the region, compared even with European efforts in scholarship and knowledge of Asia.

The origins of the American involvement, in particular, may help to explain why it has seldom been possible to think usefully about a broad "Pacific Basin" approach to the region. To be sure, some scholars and visionaries—often as a point of rhetorical departure—have conceptualized the region in those terms, but so broad a concept of the "Pacific Basin" has seldom related closely to actual behavior. Our patterns of thought are more often found to be shaped not within a broad, positive and regionwide framework, but within the narrower and more apprehensive context of two-nation relations. And it is even more evident that Americans, when they are asked to think in terms of the "Pacific," tend most readily to think specifically in terms of the American relationship with Japan. For Japan is the feature of the "Pacific Basin" concept which appears most clearly to have an immediate and pragmatic impact upon the United States—in the past for reasons of defense and security, and for the present and forseeable future for reasons of economics as well as political security.

This suggests that American thinking is still heavily informed by a negative or defensive posture toward the Pacific at a time when the relative and perhaps declining role of the United States in world affairs may call for a considerably more constructive and wide-ranging style. This is not to underestimate the major impact of Japan's behavior on so many aspects of Pacific Basin affairs. It is simply to recognize instead that neither the United States nor Japan is likely to dominate the region, and to recognize as well that the interests of both Japan and the U.S. probably will be enhanced by forms of positive participation in a "Pacific Basin" that increasingly is widely construed in reality as well as in rhetoric.

It is clear from what has been said already that there is really no body which speaks with a single voice for the nations of the Pacific Basin. There are, of course, several regional organizations concerned with specialized aspects of the area, such as the Asian Development Bank (ADB), United Nations Economic Commission for Asia and the Far East (ECAFE) and the Association of Southeast Asian Nations (ASEAN). However, these organizations are either not concerned with economic policy or strategic matters for all nations which are in or which border the Pacific, or they are concerned with very narrow quasi-economic matters. Basically, economic and political policy for the area is set by the dictates of a few giants which operate in the area; policies of the major players set the tune to which the small countries adjust. The Pacific area has been one where national interests clearly precede international cooperation.

The new politico-economic policy for the Pacific Basin inevitably must concern itself with:

1. differing rates of economic growth and widening gaps in wealth and income;
2. uncoordinated trade policies of trade liberalization here, mixed with growing protectionism there;
3. the role of uncertainty in foreign investment controls which encourage or hamper international flows of resources under some theme of nationalism or as a reaction to fears created by multinational enterprises;
4. governmental interaction seen largely through official flows of financial resources to correct imagined or real economic imbalances although basically concerned with winning political points;
5. great uncertainties regarding the future political and strategic roles of one giant in the area—the United States—and almost total ignorance about the likely role of potential giants in this realm—Japan, China and even the Soviet Union; and
6. continuing political instabilities, caused in part by unresolved growth and development problems, that can lead once more to outbreaks of so-called "internal wars."

The widening gap between the rich and poor is starker and more strongly felt in Asia than elsewhere in the world. Despite a trend in Asia and the Pacific toward greater self-reliance, political pragmatism and economic realism, national efforts have not been successful in relieving hunger or effecting more equitable distributions of income. The largest rice shortage in many years took place in 1972, due partly to natural disasters, but also to human miscalculation. Shortfalls in 1973 and 1974 were intensified by rapidly increasing prices of fertilizers and scarce petroleum supplies. In the Philippines, flood, and in Indonesia, drought reduced expected crops drastically. The Green Revolution has not been successful in meeting increased demands for foodstuffs.

The event which took the United Kingdom into the European Economic Community forced several Commonwealth countries to turn more actively to the Pacific region in trading relationships. Australia turned to the Pacific countries for expanding trade opportunities, reducing tariff barriers to goods from developing countries and stepping up its aid support. Australia, which has long been a dominant force in the South Pacific, was joined in its aid efforts by other developers, particularly Japan. Japan, of course, was already a strong investor in Australian mineral exploitation, as well as in Latin American countries. Among the South Pacific countries, Papua New Guinea and the Solomon Islands have also engaged in extensive mineral exploration, largely under foreign auspices. In Fiji the tourist industry, which is perhaps the simplest field to exploit, began to expand at a rapid rate; while in Western Samoa new timber explorations were being financed by international investment. These examples of new ventures show an increasing interlocking of the resources of the Pacific Basin.

Because of regional groupings in Europe and elsewhere, countries normally exporting there sought out new markets. The Pacific countries directed efforts to locating new markets, especially in Latin America; for example, New Zealand dairy imports now account for 90 percent of the Peruvian market, and in Chile they now account for 50 percent of the market. New Zealand has also found strong markets for beef and sheep in Japan.

The growing interdependence of the Pacific region has not been necessarily a multilateral effort. What used to be considered as the ugly American in Asia is being replaced by the ugly Japanese. But this situation has not developed without bitter conflicts between the old and new contenders for the title. Tokyo in many instances has refused to give way meekly to the demands of Western industrial states in order to ease the strains on the U.S. dollar, the pound or the franc, or to accommodate weakened American success in trade. By submitting to these demands Japan would abort its embryonic relationship with Asia and the Pacific. Japan is properly concerned about its image and functions in the region. On the other hand, it has had to face, on several embarrassing and harsh occasions, the resentment to Japanese economic imperialiam being voiced in Manila, Kuala Lumpur, Jakarta and Canberra.

A rising tide of resentment is being expressed in Southeast Asia against Japanese goods and investments. Boycott campaigns against Japanese imports have taken place in Thailand and Indonesia. In the Philippines, the trade treaty has been postponed, largely because of general suspicions in the Philippines of Japanese motives. Complaints have been voiced that Japanese loans and terms are too strict and are invariably tied to purchasing Japanese goods at high prices. Interest rates for Japanese aid money are several percentage points above European levels of interest for similar purposes.

In Singapore, there are criticisms of Japanese companies because Japanese nationals usually receive the higher level jobs. Japanese businessmen are not well liked in South Korea. The Indonesian National Development Agency has lodged protests claiming that Japanese aid and joint venture projects essentially benefit Japan and not the recipient country.

While Japan has incurred resentment in many countries of the Pacific and Asia, it has bent over backwards to win the favor of China. Japanese businessmen go to extreme limits to win contracts from Peking, slicing profit margins to the bone, with exports for fertilizer being a notorious example.

Although Japanese business interests have intruded deeply into most of the developing countries of the Pacific, Japanese economic might is carefully screened from international intrusion into the homeland. Despite the massive injections of U.S. capital into Japan since 1949, only in 1972 did the Japanese permit 100 percent foreign-owned subsidiaries in Japanese industry, and then only for a restricted list of industries. The existence of thousands of tiny enterprises in Japan, many of which act as subcontractors for giant conglomerates, survives mostly because of the lack of significant foreign competition domestically. At the same time, the paternalistic structures enable the country to face the twin economic terrors of inflation and unemployment with greater equanimity than other industrialized countries. Massive subsidies paid to farmers in order to develop Japanese self-sufficiency in food represent an uneconomic drain on public expenditures, thereby distorting the economy and limiting funds needed for social services and environmental improvement. Japan could well afford to lower tariffs and administrative restrictions which keep other Asian goods out of Japanese markets.

The Pacific scene is a mixture of minor national irritations and major international interdependencies. European voices no longer dominate and the American preference is to become muted. The area is the scene of a gigantic struggle for national recognition and domestic identity as well as hesitant new steps to provide acceptable leadership in the international arena. The grandiose schemes of the Japanese Greater Co-prosperity Sphere and of Sukarno's regional leadership are now replaced with a more tempered approach to fill the vacuums that the United States claims to have made in dominance over the area. Conflicts from which emerge cooperation can be found within the nations of the Pacific as well as between them. There is, hopefully, growing recognition that forms of international cooperation, perhaps most pragmatically on a regional level, can help overcome the difficulties which generate national conflict. Up to now, this recognition has largely been at the level of concept and rhetoric; the next decade will witness whether this conceptualization can be transformed into reality.

Chapter Two

The U.S. View of the Pacific Problem

Richard A. Ericson, Jr.

About twenty years ago we were talking about nothing but the "Sino-Soviet bloc" and today we talk only of the "Sino-Soviet split." The reasons for that split have been spelled out in the newspapers: the ideological controversy; the sudden pullout of technicians and Soviet support from China in the late 1950s; the border and territorial disputes; and a whole succession of subsequent events that have deepened the rift to the point where its depth is now seismic. The Sino-Soviet rift is, I think, probably the fundamental faultline on the world's diplomatic crust, and it is likely to stay that way.

More important is the fact that the U.S.S.R. and China both act on the assumption that this one-time alliance cannot be repaired, and each of them is making decisions and taking actions which tend to make reconciliation even less likely. The more that both China and the U.S.S.R. find that they are bene-fiting from growing ties with the United States, Japan and Europe, in terms of trade and technical cooperation and in terms of reduced danger of conflict, the less reason they have for restoring an alliance which never did them much good anyway. Moreover, the Chinese policy is based on a deep and abiding fear of Soviet power, which the Chinese see as surrounding and threatening them. To the north, they see forty-one Soviet nuclear equipped divisions; to the west, they see the U.S.S.R. itself; to the south, a growing Soviet influence, particularly in the Indian Ocean area; to the east, a growing Soviet fleet; and overhead, Soviet space vehicles. China also feels that the Soviet Union is encouraging and support-ing elements within China which oppose the Peking government. There are other factors, of course, which influence China's foreign policy. There is China's internal economic and political situation which has made Peking more willing to venture out into the world in recent months. There is China's quest for Taiwan. There is desire to lead the developing nations, and so on, but the fear of the Soviet Union seems to be, by far, the largest factor in determining China's foreign policy today.

THE UNITED STATES AND CHINA

Peking and Washington seem to have equally strong reasons for seeking a better dialogue and a better relationship, although their respective motives differ considerably.

American motives are:

1. to decrease tension;
2. to alleviate misunderstandings in the international arena;
3. to draw the P.R.C. into the international mainstream;
4. to accelerate Peking's trend away from extremism; and
5. to pursue certain tactical policies.

The administration wants to pursue a policy which clearly has widespread domestic political support and which thus strengthens the president's hand in the total conduct of foreign policy. Also, of course, there is the prospect that by improving relations with China we can also improve our leverage with the Soviet Union.

China's motives are somewhat different. Its leaders want primarily to counteract the Soviet threat and they have concluded that China cannot afford to have both the United States and the U.S.S.R. as its enemies. China also wants to create splits, perhaps in the U.S.–Republic of China relationship, perhaps additionally in the U.S.–Japan relationship; but it primarily wishes to isolate Taiwan. Obviously, China is at a point now where it wishes to improve its own image internationally and at home, and a key element is its relationship with the U.S.

The improvement in U.S.–China relations are not something that came about suddenly. Much took place before Peking and the United States agreed on the final moves that brought relations to the stage they are today. It can be recalled that in the months and years before the president's trip to Peking we signalled our intentions by lifting our trade and travel restrictions, and by encouraging the Chinese to take notice of what we wanted to do. A new opening and an effective signal was made in 1969. The cultural revolution was then over in China, and there seemed to be a trend in China away from extremism and toward moderation and pragmatism. The president felt that we had to move very fast while this trend persisted and while Mao was still alive to give his blessing to Chou En-lai's policy of improving U.S.–Chinese relationships. Hence our resort to the rather unconventional diplomacy—the secret Kissinger trips culminating in the February 1972 visit by the president to Peking.

In the course of all of these talks, a certain degree of mutual trust emerged and was established between us. Not that we thought China had really changed its revolutionary objectives, but rather that we had learned how we could talk with each other. We learned to speak frankly and directly with the

Chinese. We learned not to gloss over differences with them, not to talk about deals or quid pro quos. We stressed principles and mutuality, and we learned that we had to live up to our undertakings. We found that we were on opposite sides of a political spectrum, and that perhaps it was an unbridgeable gulf, and we said so, in effect, in the Shanghai communique. We also found a common ground in the area of national power interests as opposed to ideology. We both found that we had a common and genuine desire to improve our relations, and despite all our differences, we did establish mechanisms for doing so. First came the ambassadorial talks in Paris; then occasional special missions to Peking, a broadening dialogue in the U.N. and elsewhere; and most recently, of course, we have had the exchange of high-level liaison missions.

There has also been a moderate increase in our nondiplomatic communications: whereas several years ago, for example, there was no U.S.–China trade, the two-way trade in 1972 was around $200−250 million, and it was expected to reach $300 million in 1973. There have also been numerous exchanges: many Americans have now visited China, including representatives of both houses of Congress; a Chinese medical group has come here, and Chinese scientists, as well as ping-pong players and acrobats, have begun to visit the U.S.

All this has been achieved without changing our official relations with the Republic of China. We still recognize that government, and we continue our defense commitment to it. We continue to expand our trade and our investments in Taiwan, and Peking accepts this situation. Peking doubtless hopes that eventually Taiwan will become diplomatically isolated and somehow will fall into Peking's hands, probably through some special arrangements which will be necessary to preserve the higher living standards of those who live on Taiwan. We do not really know what is going to happen to Taiwan, and we say that this is an issue that must be resolved peacefully, in accordance with the will of the people on both sides of the China Strait. We increasingly do believe that the resolution of this problem will be peaceful.

With all of this broadening of the U.S.–People's Republic of China dialogue, Peking's perceptions of the United States seem to be changing. Although the Chinese do not say so, we believe that China does not want the U.S. to withdraw its military power from Southeast Asia in a way that would result in the U.S.S.R. filling the vacuum. They have a slogan in China which is "Yankee go home," but it seems to be "Yankee go home, but gradually." Similarly, China did seem to want the war in Indochina to end relatively quickly, though it could not move directly contrary to Hanoi's wishes. Nevertheless, apparently it exerted some influence on Hanoi. We also believe China may be coming to recognize that there may be some advantage to Peking in the present U.S.–Japanese defense treaty. Certainly this is the best way of insuring that Japan does not become again a great military power, a prospect which Peking professes to fear very much. This does not seem a very good reason for maintaining the U.S.–Japan security treaty. It is possibly one of the worst of all reasons; but as long as the Chinese feel that way, we might as well take advantage of it. It would be unfortunate to have our military relationships with Japan begin to depend on whether the Chinese like it or not, as the case may be.

THE UNITED STATES AND JAPAN

We repeatedly say that our improving ties with China must not be at the expense of our relationship with Japan. Japan is our most significant ally. It may not be our best ally in some ways, but it is our most important ally. If our relations with Japan remain good, the prospects for peace and for progress, specifically, are very good. If our relations with Japan should ever sour, the whole structure of peace and stability in the Pacific would be undermined.

There are admittedly a number of discordant elements in our relations with Japan today that bear careful watching and careful handling. If they are not handled carefully, we could have a serious erosion of our relationships. Some of these things are the lingering Japanese concern over the so-called "Nixon shocks" of 1971, when we suddenly announced that the president would be visiting Peking, when we levied import surcharges rather suddenly against Japanese goods, when we negotiated rather tough textile import restraint levels with the Japanese, and when we sought Japanese cooperation in a major effort to retain the Nationalist Chinese seat in the U.N., only to have Dr. Kissinger arrive in Peking on the day the vote was taken. The Japanese reaction to all of these steps was that we had done things unilaterally and suddenly, without adequate consultation as might have been expected from a good reliable ally and friend.

There is a secondary problem, of course, in the trade field which is getting increasing press coverage these days. We had a deficit of $3.2 billion in our bilateral trade with Japan in 1971. This resulted in a series of measures to redress the imbalance, including the multilateral Smithsonian currency revaluation late that year. However, despite these measures, the deficit in 1972 went even higher—to over $4 billion. This led to another round of revaluations in 1973. Japan's currency has now been appreciated with respect to the dollar by about 38 percent in two years. This imbalance, of course, has not yet been corrected and it has stirred up a lot of pressure in Congress for restrictive trade measures. Should these measures pass it could be quite disastrous for the whole international community unless adequate steps are taken to reduce Japan's surplus balance.

I think Japan will take the necessary steps, because I think that the domestic political problems which the Tanaka government and his successors face will require it. My own feeling about Japan's "tremendous growth at any price" policy is that it has already created a realization in Japan that they have gone too far with it. It has created a lot of social problems.

Those who have studied Japan carefully and closely will know that the Communists have been doing some very interesting things in Japan over the last ten years. In the 1950s, the male voices screaming out of the microphone, volume turned up high—very harsh, very bitter and obviously making an ideological harangue—were those of the unsophisticated Communists. They did very badly. Today, the voice from the sound trucks in a Japanese election probably will be female; it will be appealing, talking about garbage, schools, roads, houses and hospitals, about smog, or whether your child is getting adequate medical care, and inviting all to party headquarters where any problem can be taken care of.

The Communists portray their party as the lovable party. Their handouts show smiling faces, and their pamphlets discuss the problems which touch the everyday life of the voter. They have been very clever about educating their young leadership, and their leadership is by and large young. They have brought them through a university system. They have trained them in political staff work. They have sought power through local assemblies, electing candidates of their own where they can; helping other parties to elect candidates where they cannot elect one of their own. They have greatly increased their power in local areas, and they have moved into the national scene. In the 1972 Diet election their representation grew from fourteen to thirty-eight seats. The political section of the U.S. Embassy in Tokyo predicted twenty-five seats in that election, but the Communists got thirty-eight seats—five million votes—and over 10 percent of the eligible voters for the first time in a long time. This is not to say that the Communists are a threat with only thirty-eight seats out of 481 in the Diet. It does suggest that they have pointed out the domestic political problems for the Japanese government.

If Prime Minister Tanaka could, he would have preferred to forget about foreign affairs, trade imbalances, product surpluses, Chinese adventures and the related problems, and he would have instead, attempted to correct the internal ills that the Communist party has very accurately pointed out to him as constituting the major political problems in Japan today. This is the political problem—the quality of life in Japan. It is not a question of whether Japan is in line with the Soviet Union, or the defense treaty with the United States, or whether Japan has major trade imbalances to deal with.

Prime Minister Tanaka faced intensifying domestic political problems. When his popularity sank to a low level in 1974 it was viewed with great alarm by many in the United States. Yet when he came to power in 1972, Prime Minister Tanaka was heralded as a computerized bulldozer. His status declined eventually to a level where a prime minister probably belongs in Japan: mistrusted by most of the people. Presidents are frequently mistrusted by most of the people in this country, but the Japanese prime minister is not used to having 61 percent or 65 percent of the people say they approve of everything he is doing. It is possible Prime Minister Tanaka came in with exaggerated expectations, or people had exaggerated expectations of him because he was quite different from previous prime ministers in Japan.

To draw an American parallel, Mr. Tanaka was very much like Lyndon Johnson. They were both men from the outback, Prime Minister Tanaka coming from Niigata, not exactly a cosmopolitan place to be born and raised. Both of them had, in the eyes of their fellow countrymen, a rather sketchy education: Prime Minister Tanaka never went beyond high school; Lyndon Johnson was educated in a normal school in Texas. They were both supposed to have the "common touch"—populist if you will. Primarily, however, they were both intentionally domestic political animals. Johnson received his reputation as the most effective senate leader that the United States had seen, in terms of being able to get things done and to manipulate American policies. Tanaka was at his best in dealing with domestic politics, meaning in getting people elected, and in dealing with problems of the Liberal Democratic party.

JAPANESE SECURITY ISSUES

The basic problem that we have with the Japanese is the security treaty. We have gotten to the point now where the Japanese—the government and the people—are maintaining a rather delicate balance with respect to our security treaty. The people who run Japan—the "establishment" in Japan and those who support the government—want to see U.S. power remain in the Western Pacific. Many Japanese particularly in the opposition parties, resent the U.S. bases in Japan and Okinawa and those bases which are required to support our presence in the Pacific. We have plans to reduce the base areas and to minimize the points of friction with Japan. These problems are under constant review. Some progress has been made in some areas, but in other areas we have made none. The aim is to minimize the kind of frictions that our presence gives rise to. Nevertheless, it is going to be a very tricky business because, on the one hand, the presence of our forces impinges on rising Japanese nationalism and, on the other hand, we must have, if we are to have a credible presence in that part of the world, some kind of credible force. There is no substitute, I think, for most of the bases in Japan, and in Okinawa in particular. That is part of the problem.

Another part of the problem, of course, is the nature of the security treaty itself. The maintenance of that security treaty, which has its opponents in both the United States and in Japan, is vital for both countries. The fact that it permits us to have a lot of troops in Japan or to maintain a credible force there is not one of the reasons for its necessity. The treaty to us is a very flexible document. It can operate with no forces in Japan. We do not have to have bases in Japan in order to keep it effective. Likewise, we can operate it with very large-scale forces in Japan. We can move up and down the scale of numbers very easily.

The Japanese have more difficult problems in this respect. They have all kinds of legal problems involving what happens to the base areas once we leave them. One of the reasons we are wary about leaving them is that we are never sure that we can get back if we do leave. The important thing about the treaty is its psychological effect. However, it seems, if not more important, certainly as psychologically important for Japan as it is for the United States.

From a Washington perspective, it is terribly important that people who sit not far from Washington talk about Japan as an ally. We are going to go after them on the trade issue, but we are going to go after them as an ally, not as something else. In that way, it is vital for the United States that we maintain that security treaty. It has something of the same effect in Japan as well; it makes us both approach each other as allies. We have some difficult problems, and I suggest that the way we handle them is partly determined by the formal status of our relationship. For that reason, it would be unfortunate if anything happened to the treaty.

Despite all of these and other issues, our prospects for good relations with Japan are, I think, very bright, largely because both countries realize the tremendous stake we have in maintaining that good relationship and avoiding letting it become sour.

JAPANESE-CHINESE RELATIONSHIPS

Japan has a strong desire to have close relations with the P.R.C. This has much to do with Japan's cultural heritage, its propinquity to China, racial factors, feelings of guilt over the past and, of course, the rather materialistic factors, such as China with its 850 million as a potential market for Japanese goods. We can all contemplate the Japanese safety pin manufacturer who says figuratively, "if every Chinaman would just buy one more safety pin. . . . " It is this kind of psychology.

Until recently, this desire for better Sino–Japanese relations was not reciprocated by the Chinese. In fact in Peking, after attitudes towards the United States began to change, Japan was regarded as China's public enemy number two. Many of our people who went to China at the time of the president's visit and of Dr. Kissinger's earlier visit were struck by the depth of anti-Japanese sentiments displayed there. They were showing wartime atrocity movies, anti-Japanese posters, plays, this kind of thing, and they left out no opportunity for telling our people how much they distrusted the Japanese.

However, this has changed in recent months, partly because of China's fear of the U.S.S.R. and its desire not to have more than one major enemy, and partly because of its growing awareness that U.S.-Japanese ties are not as inimical as China once thought. The fact is that the present government in Japan is also committed to a policy of greatly improved relations with China. China also has trade and material interests involved in its attitude. One can only speculate, for example, whether China was impelled to normalize its relations with Japan by the realization that if it was to modernize its terribly backward economy, one of the primary sources of technological assistance, goods and machinery would have to be Japan. It could not be the U.S.S.R., nor the United States. Europe was too remote. Japan was its only logical source. Of course, a further factor in China's considerations is Japan's relations with the Soviet Union. When President Nixon, for example, was in China, Gromyko visited Japan, and China's radio broadcasts, which were normally vituperatively anti-Japanese, suddenly quieted. It seemed clear that China did not want to drive Japan toward the U.S.S.R.; rather, it tried to woo Japan.

Japan does find itself in an enviable position in some ways between China and the Soviet Union. It does have leverage on each because of its relations with the other. An example of how these things reciprocate occurred in March 1973, when Prime Minister Tanaka sent a letter to Prime Minister Brezhnev. This was a balancing gesture, intended as such, against Japan's approaches to the Chinese. On March 6, 1973, Brezhnev received for the first time the Japanese ambassador. They had a long interview. On March 7, Peking retaliated. It announced the visit to Japan of the head of the Japan–China association, and stated that the People's Republic of China opposed Japan's assistance in Siberian development projects. The Soviets promptly denounced the P.R.C. for meddling, and Brezhnev's letter to Tanaka soon followed. This letter seems to be a centerpiece of a Soviet campaign to put a wedge between Japan and China. It invited Prime Minister Tanaka to come to Moscow at the earliest possible opportunity. Here is a sequence of events, in the space of about five weeks, in which the Soviets and the Chinese seem to alternate in attempting to woo the Japanese away from each other.

There are many people in the United States who criticized Tanaka when, in 1972, he went to Peking within several months of becoming prime minister. The critics focused on his rather unseemly haste, although I would submit that he did not go in haste at all. He had ample time to tell the president of the United States exactly what it was that he was going to do in Peking. He told us that he was 80 percent sure of what the results would be and that this estimation was based on very careful sounding by the Japanese over a number of years as to what the Chinese wanted of them.

Those who said that Tanaka went in haste do him an injustice. Largely, the United States and the Chinese themselves determined the pace and the content of this visit much more than Prime Minister Tanaka did. The real effect of President Nixon's announcement that he was going to Peking was in terms of Japanese domestic politics. The major effect of that announcement was to tremendously increase the great pressure for normalization of relations with China which was already present in Japan. The Japanese were hurt, wounded, shocked and unhappy over the way the announcement was made—especially that we did not consult with them—but this was only a small part of the problem.

The point is that there was already this tremendous pressure in Japan for Prime Minister Sato to do something about relations with Peking.

This pressure was further increased by the fact that the Chinese had said, "No, we will not deal with you, Sato," and kept saying "no" for about eight or nine months more. Then Tanaka became prime minister, and the Chinese changed overnight. If they had really been interested in meddling in Japanese domestic affairs, they had a wonderful setup for doing so. They had tremendous Japanese pressure to work with. Instead, for reasons of their own, probably related to the Soviet Union, to us and to all the rest of it, they decided to receive Prime Minister Tanaka. It was as if Tanaka was standing against the door with the whole Japanese population pushing him, and when the Chinese opened that door, he fell in.

It seems Japan has also found it advantageous to play China against the U.S.S.R. Japan is more interested in close ties with China than it is with the U.S.S.R., but by flirting with Moscow, it does gain leverage over China. Also, by moving closer to China, Japan gains some leverage over the U.S.S.R. In the latter respect, I think the Japanese learned primarily from us.

JAPAN AND THE SOVIET UNION

What does Japan seek to gain from an improved relationship with Moscow? For one thing, of course, there is the recovery of the four island groupings, which lie to the north of Japan and are visible from Japan itself. The Soviets occupied these islands after World War II, and this dispute is the primary reason why they have not signed a peace treaty. (It must be remembered that they have had full diplomatic relations and a great deal of trade since the middle of 1950.) Unlike Okinawa, there are no Japanese living on any of these islands, but no Japanese government can survive the signing away of any of them, and any Japanese government must insist on their return. Moscow, of course, is unwilling to return them at all, for this would set a dangerous precedent for Moscow's dealings with similar territorial problems with the Chinese and Eastern Europeans. This remains a stalemate. I do not see any real prospect that either the Japanese or the Soviets will change their position on these islands very soon.

There are also very powerful psychological constraints on the good relations between Japan and the Soviet Union. They have been traditional enemies over the centuries. Japan's memories of the Soviet's aggressive behavior at the end of World War II are very keen, and there are, moreover, thousands of Japanese families who are affected deeply by the Soviet refusal to account for thousands of Japanese prisoners who disappeared after World War II in Siberian labor camps. There were thousands and thousands of Japanese who surrendered to the Soviet Union shortly after World War II, and many thousands of them did not come home. The Soviets have not accounted for many of them. Anybody who has ever served in an American embassy or consulate abroad knows the

Japanese fixation, the tremendous psychological pressure on the Japanese, to know where the remains of their missing people are. I would not be very much surprised if, right now, there are not at least five or six Japanese missions wandering around the trust territories of the Pacific, the Philippines or somewhere else in Southeast Asia looking for the remains of Japanese. This view comes as a complete surprise to the Soviets. If something is over, and gone, and passed, they do not want to talk about it. Nevertheless, the difference in approach is going to be a problem to both countries.

One test of just how incompatible are the social, political and economic systems of Japan and the Soviets may come in connection with the familiar talk of joint Siberian development. Recently, the Soviets have appeared to be more flexible on this subject, which may represent a break from the past. Throughout the late fifties and sixties there seems to have been a pattern of enticement on this subject, usually reflected when the Soviets and the Japanese determined their trade in a series of annual discussions. It always seemed that just before these discussions were going to convene, the Soviets would be interested in talking about the Japanese coming into Siberia and doing a little development work. As the date of the negotiations approached, these discussions, this enticement, would become more and more active, but after the trade discussions were over, the subject would die. Next year, three or four months before the trade discussions convened again, it would be raised again.

Lately, in contrast, the Soviets seem to have become a little more flexible toward the Japanese. The pattern of enticement is no longer quite what it was, and both countries seem to be serious about a joint Siberian effort. The Soviets have reason now to want to tie Siberia together. They have the Chinese threat, and they do not have the capital for Siberia's development.

Japan does, and Japan is also driven by an energy hunger. This is what the Japanese are interested in; they want to develop energy resources and are looking pretty far ahead. They know that in the 1980s, even if these Siberian resources were fully developed, they could satisfy only perhaps 10 percent of Japan's energy needs at that time. Yet that is an important 10 percent.* It is a diversified 10 percent, for one thing. Thus, the Japanese are very anxious to get into these energy products in Siberia, but they also need American participation.

CONCLUSIONS

Despite the thaws in the cold war, a equilibrium in Eastern Asia assumes that the major powers of the world continue to have objectives similar to those they had in the past—though today they pursue these objectives less through bluster, adventure and war, and more through diplomacy and subtle splitting tactics. Of

Editor's note: Mr. Ericson's prescient emphasis on Japan's "energy hunger" has of course been acutely re-emphasized by the steep rise in price of Middle Eastern oil in 1974.

course, they retain their ability to influence the actions of the minor powers, but the means are not always clear, and their influence seems to have declined somewhat recently. It is certainly less than it was during the Cold War days, when the world seemed to be divided into two major blocs.

Today, in contrast, the influence of the great powers seems primarily to be in the direction of halting wars in which they might themselves become involved. To put this proposition another way is to say that the great powers are increasingly averse to upsetting the equilibrium of forces in the world. Thus, China wants us out of Southeast Asia, but it does not want us out in a way that brings the Soviets into Southeast Asia to fill the vacuum left by our departure. Similarly, the Soviets probably do not want us out of Southeast Asia in a way that would allow the Chinese to fill that vacuum.

Certainly, both the Soviets and Chinese would have reasons to be disturbed if the U.S. were to pull its forces out of the Western Pacific. This would dangerously upset the present equilibrium and lead to new dangers. The Japanese see this point. They realize that the presence of U.S. forces in the Western Pacific is much more palatable to our adversaries than was once the case. Our bases are not provocative centers as the Japanese had once thought they were, nor are they lightning rods. They help to preserve the almost universally desired goal in East Asia of a local equilibrium.

Given Japan's great and growing economic power and the basic identity of our systems and our goals, we have no recourse but to operate in a multipolar world, in closest possible association with Japan. This may require more skill, more expertise and more effort than we have recently been able to bring to bear on it, because it is not an easy problem. We speak frequently of the interrelationship, the interdependence of the United States and Japan. We talk about the great web of associations that we have woven since the end of World War II, and the tremendous trade we have between our two countries, which already surpasses anything in foreign trade that the world has ever seen and is growing very fast. Despite the tremendous imbalance that we have, Japan is our largest and fastest-growing overseas market. Of course, we, too, provide a tremendous market for the kind of sophisticated goods that the Japanese want more and more to produce.

We speak of all of our cultural ties, exchanges of visitors, our identity of interests and all the rest of it, but we really deal with each other across a tremendous cultural gap. We are going to be rivals and we are going to be competitors as much as we are going to be partners and allies in the future. It does not take a genius to realize, when you project the kind of growth that Japan has experienced (although it will probably not grow as fast as it has in the future), that in absolute terms Japanese growth is going to continue to be astounding. It is going to continue to bring us into rivalry and competition for markets and for raw material sources all over the world, including those in the United States.

These issues force us to realize that it will require great understanding on both sides, great understanding of each other's domestic and political situations. Indeed, when it comes to that, I think Dr. Kissinger said the truest thing that can be said about this kind of problem: "The proper way to conduct an alliance is to know what your ally's domestic political problems are and to behave accordingly." That is the kind of understanding that we are going to have to have of Japan, and that Japan is going to have to have of us. Each of us is going to have to develop and maintain a solid and mutual understanding of the other's motives and intentions, and as Dr. Kissinger said, "behave accordingly."

Chapter Three

A Japanese View of the Pacific Problem

Masao Sawaki

Japan and the United States—because of their differences, their similarities and their fundamental common interests—are bound to have occasional conflicts of interest. But for the very same reasons they are also destined to be partners, cooperating closely in the pursuit of common goals. Both are democracies and major Pacific powers. The two are also the ranking economic powers in the free world. And they are the only two nations whose vital national interests as trading powers are global in scope.

The United States has become the paramount global economic power in recent history.

Yours was the only intact, surplus-producing economy in the world at the end of the war. You generously undertook unprecedented responsibilities for reconstructing the world economy, financing international development and underwriting free-world security. You were chief architects of the world monetary system, and you provided the impetus for liberalizing world trade. As a result, the world has benefited in recent decades from the greatest expansion of trade—and of world economic growth—in history.

Japan has become a global economic power principally through its worldwide trade.

Unlike the richly endowed United States, Japan is virtually without essential natural resources of raw materials and fuels, and with insufficient available land to feed its people. With a population half that of the United States crowded into an area about the size of California, Japan must reach out to the Middle East and Southeast Asia for its petroleum; to East Asia and the Western Hemisphere for its lumber; to Asia, Oceania, Africa and the Americas for its minerals; to the United States for a wide variety of industrial raw materials, as well as foods and fibers, especially grains; and to all the oceans of the world for fish, a staple of the Japanese diet.

It is Japan's absolute dependence on imports that has made it necessary for us to become successful exporters. We must export to pay for our essential imports. But the foundation for Japan's economic growth has been the fast-growing Japanese domestic market, rather than foreign trade.

In this respect we are also very much like the United States. In fact, of all the industrialized nations, our two countries depend less on foreign trade than any other—around 5 percent of GNP for the United States and about 10 percent for Japan.

Over the long run, as both our economies have grown and prospered they have also meshed in a complementary way. The United States has been for nearly a century Japan's largest customer and supplier. And, for the United States, Japan has been in recent decades your largest overseas customer, and your most diversified customer for farm and factory products, as well as for raw materials.

During these postwar decades—for political as well as for economic reasons—Japan, at least, developed a strong sense of interdependence with the United States. In American eyes, however, our relationship began to assume a slightly different coloration by the early 1960s, in response to Japan's extremely rapid economic growth and a corresponding expansion of Japanese trade.

In the communique of the Japan–U.S. joint cabinet conference of 1961, the relationship was already being described as an "equal partnership." In Japan this was interpreted to mean that, fifteen years after the war, Japan was once again on its own feet and no longer needed a special client relationship with the United States. By 1972 President Nixon, in his foreign policy message to Congress, was announcing "a movement away from the rigid bipolarism of the 1940s and 1950s toward a more fluid and heterogeneous, multipolar international order." In this new order the two superpowers, the United States and the Soviet Union, were now joined by growing centers of economic power in Western Europe, Japan and China.

In the meantime, the growth of Japanese exports to the United States—and the development of an American trade and payments deficit with Japan and other countries—was adding fuel to protectionist fires in the United States. A big share of this fire has been directed against Japan.

This was also the period when Japan experienced what we call the "Nixon shocks." The first shock came in the spring of 1971 when, without any prior consultation with Japan, President Nixon announced his plan to visit the People's Republic of China. In the summer of 1971 the president again surprised Japan and the world with the announcement of his "New Economic Policy." This policy had the effect of suspending the rules of the world monetary system, a situation that still has not been resolved.

Japanese use the word "shock" not simply in the sense of "surprise," but more because these events shocked the Japanese people into a realization that the relationship with the United States has undergone a profound change. There has been a loss of intimacy and closeness of consultation. Even the very welcome reversion of Okinawa in the spring of 1971 failed to offset this shaking of Japan's confidence in the specialness of the relationship.

Indeed, the first Nixon shock had considerable impact on domestic Japanese politics. It hastened the fall of the Sato cabinet, and made it imperative that the first order of business of the new Tanaka cabinet was normalization of relations with China. The Japanese people understood that the change in the relationship meant that Japan must now develop greater independence in the pursuit of its national interest.

Yet the change has clearly *not* meant in Japanese eyes any lessening of cooperation with the United States. On the contrary, the overlapping interests and common goals of the two countries continue to require close and friendly consultation, and careful coordination of policies. I can illustrate this point by commenting on our parallel interests in three areas—trade, foreign investment and aid to the developing countries.

For the first fifteen years following the war, Japan had a deficit in our two-way trade. Eight years ago—in 1965—the deficit shifted to the United States. Last year's $4.1 billion U.S. deficit with Japan was nearly two-thirds of the overall U.S. trade deficit.

This turnaround coincided with two trends which put our economies out of phase with each other. One was the very rapid and efficient expansion of the Japanese economy, which kept unit labor costs down despite large increases in manufacturing wages. The competitiveness of Japanese exports in world markets actually improved during the second half of the sixties. The opposite trend was the sluggishness of the U.S. economy during those same years, where inflation and lagging productivity increased unit labor costs. U.S. exports became progressively less competitive during this period.

The recent currency realignments were designed to compensate for this situation—especially the nearly 30 percent upward valuation of the yen in relation to the dollar. In fact, as the recent economic report of the president indicates, unit labor costs measured in the new currency values have risen less in the United States since 1965 than in some other major trading countries. The U.S. rise was 26 percent, compared to 30 percent in the U.K., 44 percent in Japan, 61 percent in Italy and 80 percent in West Germany at the end of last year.

The effects of the currency realignments are also beginning to show up in trade. For example, Japanese exports to the United States of automobiles, textiles, iron and steel products, and TV sets actually decreased in quantity in 1972, although the dollar value rose somewhat because of price increases under yen revaluation. In fact, during the winter quarter—December through February—U.S. imports from Japan grew by only 16.6 percent, while U.S. exports to Japan jumped 42 percent over the same period in the previous year.

These are welcome developments in Japan as well as the United

States, since it is in our common interest to bring this trade back into reasonable balance. In this spirit, Japan has taken bolder and more decisive steps than any other U.S. trading partner, over the past two years, to help improve your export performance. These have included unilateral tariff cuts and the removal of nontariff barriers, which make Japan now a much less-protected market than the United States—and one of the most accessible and promising markets in the world for expanded U.S. exports.

Another important factor which is helping us toward our common goal of a better balanced trade is the transformations now under way in the Japanese domestic society. Rising per capita incomes and increased leisure are creating a boom in all types of consumer goods, services and recreation. These demands cannot be fully satisfied by domestic production. As a result, 1972 imports of durable consumer goods were 76.2 percent higher than in 1971. This astonishing growth in import demand is a potential bonanza for enterprising American exporters who study the Japanese market and tastes, adapt their products accordingly and do an aggressive selling job. The customers are there, waiting!

Another transformation is under way as Japan pays increased attention to social and quality-of-life problems such as cleaning up the environment, building adequate housing, and providing more roads, hospitals, public services and utilities. These are all important needs which were sacrificed in our headlong rush toward high economic growth in the late 1950s and 1960s. We can no longer postpone action. But once again, domestic Japanese production is inadequate to meet demand. We will have to import technology, materials and capital goods to accomplish what is necessary to the welfare of the Japanese people. This too means an expanding opportunity for American exporters.

The rewards for seizing these opportunities in the Japanese market can be very lucrative. An editorial in the March 1973 issue of *Fortune* magazine suggests that the United States could double its export of goods and services to Japan by 1976, and provide a million new American jobs in the process. It is possible that Japan could become America's largest foreign customer for both consumer and industrial goods. Such effort, it is rightly pointed out, would require more American initiative and the right kind of salesmanship.

I am optimistic, in other words, about the long-term outlook for better balanced Japanese-American trade. There are domestic challenges on each side—from inflation to social reconstruction—which each country will have to deal with in its own way. Fortunately, however, these distinct domestic priorities are actually complementary as they affect our trade with each other. It is important, therefore, that we also make our trade policies complementary and compatible.

The world has had enough experience, particularly since the 1930s, to know that the wrong way to try to solve trade problems is to restrict imports, which has the effect of reducing trade. The right way is to seek a balance at higher levels of trade, by expanding exports from the deficit country.

The periods of greatest trade expansion in recent years have also been periods of strong economic growth for the United States, Japan and other major trading nations. National prosperity and international prosperity are two aspects of the same healthy process.

Since the United States and Japan are the two largest free-enterprise economies in the world, it is understandable that entrepreneurs in both our countries share a great enthusiasm for the future of multinational investment. The Europeans may have invented the multinational enterprise, but you Americans have carried the concept to significant world dimensions. Cumulative direct U.S. foreign investment, if equated with GNP, is now the tenth largest "economy" in the world.

Japan's direct foreign investments are more modest, since we have only begun to accumulate significant foreign reserves and investment capacity. However, the rate of new Japanese investment multiplied ten times in the last decade and there is every reason to believe it will continue to grow dramatically. Appreciation of the yen over the past sixteen months will help. Moreover, the $6 billion current value of our overseas holdings represents only about 2 percent of Japan's GNP, compared to 7 or 8 percent for most European nations. Since Western Europe and Japan are at comparable stages of economic development, there is a good deal of room for Japan to accelerate its investment outflow.

There are four basic reasons for Japan's increasing participation in the economies of other nations.

First is Japan's concern, as the world's largest importer of raw materials, with assuring adequate sources of supply. Thus, over 30 percent of current Japanese foreign investment is in mining and oil extraction.

Second, Japan is now exporting the production of goods which can no longer be manufactured economically in Japan. Ours is no longer a cheap labor economy; wages are now on a par with those in England and France, and are rising on an average 15 percent a year. As a result, more than 50 percent of our overseas investment in manufacturing is in the lower wage countries of East, South and Southeast Asia. Latin America ranks second. Fortunately our self-interest coincides with the needs of these nations to modernize their economies, expand jobs and increase exports.

Third, by diverting a portion of its new manufacturing investment abroad—to developed as well as developing areas—Japan can direct a larger portion of its national energies and limited resources to improving the environment and expanding the social capital of Japanese society. As I indicated earlier, this policy will also promote imports from the United States and other countries, and contribute to balancing our bilateral trade accounts.

Finally, foreign investment—especially in advanced countries like the

United States—helps secure Japan's position in major markets where our future access may be threatened by protectionism. This, of course, is a business strategy familiar to American multinationals, including those operating inside the European community. The foreign investment policies and practices of Japan and the United States, in other words, are already in perfect harmony.

Let me turn now from investment to foreign aid. Japan began very early to follow the U.S. lead by establishing aid and technical assistance ties with East and Southeast Asia, and more recently, with all the developing regions of the world. Japan now ranks second only to the United States as an aid donor. In 1971 Japan's aid amounted to $2.1 billion, or 0.96 percent of GNP, which is close to the 1 percent recommended UN target.

By far the largest part of Japan's official development aid—over 98 percent in 1971—still goes to Asia, and over 51 percent of this to Southeast Asia. As a result, Japan's economic aid commitments already exceed those of the United States in the Philippines, Thailand, Burma, Malaysia and Singapore. We are about evenly matched in Indonesia, where each supplies one-third of all that country's aid. In the Republic of Korea, Japan will pass the United States as the principal aid source in the very near future.

Japan is now rapidly expanding its aid to other areas, such as Africa and Latin America. Long-term development loans have been committed to Peru, Mexico and Paraguay in Latin America; to Iran in the Near East; and in Africa to Ethiopia, Kenya, Tanzania, Uganda and Nigeria. Commitments of untied aid have already been made to Burma and Indonesia, and a similar agreement is being negotiated with Thailand. The untying of aid means, of course, that some of this money will no doubt be used to purchase U.S. exports. We warmly support the spread of this practice of untying aid.

Japan is also vigorously increasing its subscriptions and contributions to multilateral agencies. Our contributions to the Asian Development Bank exceed those of the United States, and over the past three years Japan has channeled $1.3 billion to the International Bank for Reconstruction and Development in the form of contributions, loans and yen bonds.

An important by-product of this expanding Japanese aid effort is that it supplements and reinforces the support the United States has long provided to the development of the third world. We are sharing the burden with you because our goal is the same—a more stable, prosperous and peaceful world.

So, in the final analysis, there are many more reasons for cooperation than for conflict between Japan and the United States.

There are so many striking parallels between our two countries—in our common commitment to free enterprise, as well as to political democracy; in our global outlook and our mutual stake in building a more stable and dynamic world economy; and increasingly in our parallel interests in international investment and development assistance.

In my opinion, no other two great industrial powers are closer in their vital national interests and goals than Japan and the United States—despite the great disparity in our size and power, and the great differences in our histories and cultures.

Ours is indeed a unique partnership, with a great creative potential for the world and the future.

Chapter Four

Conflict and Cooperation: Japan and America

Robert W. Barnett

"New Political Economy in the Pacific" suggests system, and system suggests, to me, some certainties. Instead, there are today, I fear, almost universal uncertainties, about the security intentions and undertakings of the major countries; about the importance of IMF and GATT rules to the international monetary and commercial system; about likely United States responses to requests for military and economic assistance; and about what is "ideological" in economic and military confrontations within the area. These uncertainties deprive us of the comfort of relying on the old or really perceiving the outlines of anything new.

Some will look for a causal connection between all this and President Nixon's intentions and so-called doctrines. But the causes of the changes we see are deeper and only partially influenced by Washington.

The changing panorama of the Pacific region can be attributed, I believe, to three structural developments. We cannot discuss the quality and prospect of United States–Japanese relations without first identifying them.

First is the enmity between Moscow and Peking which, perceptible a decade earlier, was revealed in chilling degree during the spring and summer of 1969. None can speak usefully today of a collective communist confrontation with the so-called free world.

Second is Japan's seemingly invincible and interminable competitive capability in the world economy, properly recognized only in 1967, when Japan began to run its balance of payments surplus on bilateral account with the United States.

Third was the revelation during 1968 that the American electorate was weary of the premises upon which its best and brightest had conducted or wished to conduct American national affairs, at home and abroad, over most of the past thirty years.

I suggest that President Nixon really had very little to do with bringing about these structural changes. He responded to them and exploited them with flair and political dexterity. He did not create the pentagonal world, in which the emerging Japan was one actor: he merely recognized the existence of a new situation in which Washington could no longer stay in control.

As a result of these developments, our two countries need each other. We are, in fact, utterly indispensable to each other. Conflicts between Washington and Tokyo can all be seen to have been tactical, and they will continue to be. Cooperation has been, and will continue to be, strategic. And the challenge to statesmanship in Washington and Tokyo will be to distinguish properly between what is tactical and what strategic.

For the coming decade the United States will be strong on the world scene in ways that Japan can never be strong, and should not try to be strong. For example, an attempt by Japan to create for itself showdown military capabilities would very likely reduce rather than increase the safety of Japan and its neighborhood. Meanwhile, over the coming decade Japan will be gaining greater economic powers during a period while the United States will most likely be looking for ways to serve national interests, both in what it does at home and as a participant in the world community.

Saying this, and believing that more and more Japanese and American leaders share in this overview, let me mention several areas of conflict. These include problems like initial attitudes toward Okinawa reversion, textiles export quotas, adjustments in the international monetary system, Washington's surprise tactics in seeking detente with Peking and the Vietnam settlement.

As my examples of cooperation, I will discuss Tokyo's friendly acquiescence in the American use of Japanese bases for United States global strategic purposes, our pursuit of common policies with respect to arms control, the establishment of the Asian Development Bank, our participation in the multilateral assistance program for Indonesia, the tendency toward a merging of our interests and intentions in creating economic links with Peking and Moscow, increasingly liberal investment policies—including United States access to Japan and encouragement of Japanese capital outflows, even to the United States—and development of consultative processes, both governmental and private, more diversified and frequent than we have with any other country in the world.

Okinawa reversion brought an end to the post–World War II and post-"occupation" compromise of Japanese sovereignty inherent in the administration by Americans of islands belonging to Japan but used by United States forces for Washington's strategic and logistic purposes. With strong Japanese public demand rising in the background, Tokyo and Washington accomplished "reversion" on terms that ultimately satisfied Japanese amour propre, while preserving military facilities on the Ryukyus vital for United States strategic undertakings in the Western Pacific and reinforcing Japanese public acceptance of American military persons and facilities on the Japanese home islands.

In the concluding phases of an otherwise masterful display on both sides of diplomatic tact, foresight and realism in accomplishing "reversion," two misunderstandings arose that were to haunt the two countries for several years.

The first of these came from Washington's success in obtaining from Japan a declaration that it had a security interest in South Korea and in the Taiwan Strait. Japan was obliged to engage in awkward explanations of how the Nixon–Sato Communique of 1969 might be reconciled with Japan's overall policy of denying itself a military role beyond defense of the home islands. Prime Minister Tanaka's visit to Peking in September 1972 changed the general situation and seems to have ended interest in that possible misunderstanding.

The second misunderstanding arising from Okinawa reversion was, alas, a breakdown of communications, personally between Prime Minister Sato and President Nixon over an apparent irrelevancy: textile quotas. President Nixon believed Prime Minister Sato had promised something which no Japanese Prime Minister had the power to deliver. Supposing that "Japan, Incorporated" made it possible for a Prime Minister to override Diet, industry and labor interests whenever necessary, President Nixon believed that Prime Minister Sato had been guilty of bad faith. Months of simmering irritation and occasional bursts of overt rage characterized repeated confrontations between the two countries on textiles. In the end, Japan bent to Washington's demands, though deeply resentful of the American bullying. The conflict had been real, but the issue in statistical terms had been, right along, a trivial element in the overall frame of United States–Japanese economic relations. Though it would be stretching a point to say textiles are forgotten, they are no longer a subject producing angry talk.

Emotions were aroused, again, by Henry Kissinger's surprising visit to Peking. For months, indeed for years, Washington had promised to keep Tokyo fully informed on China developments. It had badgered Tokyo to conform to Washington's policies of nonrecognition, strategic trade embargo, support of Taiwan and general ostracism of the People's Republic of China from the world community. On July 15, 1971 came the first great "Nixon shock." Today conflict between Washington and Tokyo on China policy appears to have been tactical, however intense the emotionalism that went into Tokyo's charges of Washington's bad faith. Tanaka could never have gone to Peking had Nixon not gone first.

The president's August 15, 1971 10 percent import surcharge announcement shocked and hurt Tokyo. Again, bad faith was charged. Actually, Japanese leaders within the government and in business circles knew that they could not fairly claim to have been kept in ignorance of Washington's growing alarm about its balance of payments outlook and its intention to adopt needed remedies. In fact, Tokyo grudgingly praised Washington's attempts to strengthen the dollar: clearly such an effort was in the long-term interest of a predominantly dollar-dependent Japanese economy. Although there has been some quarrelsomeness about gold, revaluation, devaluation, fixed versus floating exchange rates, and so forth and so on, between American and Japanese negotiators, Japan proved itself to be the most forthcoming and substantial contributor of any major country to the Smithsonian Agreement, which was sought by the United States in December 1971, and the most responsive and responsible participant in continuing adjustment with the February 12 dollar devaluation. Thus, although there was conflict over detail, the common achievement served strategic interests of both countries.

Washington has charged Japan with manifold and sinister protectionism to keep American exports out of the Japanese market. Tokyo has charged Washington with insistence upon need for voluntary Japanese export controls, taking little account of factors in Japanese domestic politics which it would be unthinkable for an American politician to disregard. Still, even the most aggravating of these disputes has had a way of being overcome by good sense, and ultimate recognition of the vital complementary character of the two countries.

For the past three or four years, or longer, Japanese leaders have wanted to play a significant role in the reconstruction of Indochina when it would be possible to do this without involvement in the war or in cold war confrontation. Ignoring or scorning this caveat, Washington condemned Tokyo for not giving more aid for Laos, South Vietnam and Cambodia. But then, as ceasefire, settlement and a Paris conference loomed in sight, the White House seemed to accept without great struggle Hanoi's veto of Japanese participation in postwar planning for Indochina. Japan was not invited to Paris. This disappointed Tokyo. However, it could be that before long Washington and Tokyo will see that Tokyo's present noninvolvement in the rather messy transitional situation of the moment will give Japan political credentials for nonalignment and detachment which could be of great strategic value for the future.

I am suggesting, in the foregoing remarks, that particular conflicts between Washington and Tokyo have been of short duration and largely lent themselves to constructive resolution.

Against this background of observed resentments and passing rages on both sides, let me now speak of some significant areas of cooperation. These are but illustrations. Were time to permit it, the list would be much longer.

The United States holds a nuclear umbrella over Japan. And roots of pacifism in Japan of today are deep. They go back not only to Hiroshima and Nagasaki but to the total bankruptcy of the military leadership that had carried Japan first into Manchuria and China, and then to Pearl Harbor. There have been moments of ambiguity as spokesmen for the Pentagon and Japanese officials have talked about Japan's rearmament. Often these conversations seemed to reflect greater American concern with our balance of payments difficulties than with any desire to redefine strategy requirement. Notwithstanding recurring discussion of a possible Japanese military role in, for example, places like South

Korea or the Taiwan Strait, the White House and Congress are glad to see in Japan a firm and enduring commitment to the exclusively defensive stance and capability, called for by the Japanese Constitution. All Japanese governments since 1952 have adhered to a policy of nonproduction, nonpossession and nonintroduction of nuclear weapons, although the doctrine was enunciated as such only in 1968. Japan has signed the Nonproliferation Treaty, and although it has not yet ratified that treaty, it seems certain to do so. Meanwhile, in disarmament and arms control negotiations worldwide, Japanese and American negotiators support each other in significant ways.

Japan and the United States, jointly, were the architects of the Asian Development Bank. Initially, the United States seemed most likely to be the source of funds for future concessional lending and grant activity. Actually, however, the Japanese contributions to ADB Special—soft window—Funds have been large, while ours have been zero, notwithstanding repeated executive branch approaches to the Congress for needed appropriations. We now see a situation in which Japan is ready to increase enormously the use of the ADB for administration of Japanese aid funds were it not that a laggard Washington, failing to keep pace, presents Tokyo with the necessity of exercising restraint for fear of making it appear that the ADB is a creature of Japan. Meanwhile, in the management and on the executive board, Americans and Japanese work in harmony.

After the coup and countercoup of late 1965 which in due course led to the removal of Sukarno from Indonesia's political scene, President Suharto and his lieutenants demonstrated, in the international community, remarkable gifts of candor, foresight and self-discipline. Donor countries wished to help Indonesia to stabilize and reconstruct the economic system which Sukarno's administration had left in ruins. Jakarta wisely decided to choose international agencies like the World Bank and the IMF, and some kind of multilateral aid supervising group to lean on, rather than to depend on the United States or any other single country. Before aid could be seriously considered there was need for a debt settlement. In the years from 1966 to 1973, the Japanese record within the multilateral context was extraordinary. Prime Minister Sato, for example, was the first to tell Dr. Hermann Abs that Japan would support Dr. Abs' radical recommendations for settlement of the Sukarno debt. Moreover, for Indonesia Japan broke through many traditional barriers as it extended program loans, untied aid and made available funds to Indonesian credit institutions. Indonesia benefitted greatly from the very close relationship which developed between Washington and Tokyo in this common endeavor.

For many years Tokyo has pursued a foreign economic policy which "separated politics from economics." This meant that Tokyo often found it difficult or unpleasant to go along with the "strategic trade" controls which the United States wished to apply to China, Russia, North Korea, North Vietnam and Cuba. Tokyo cooperated, but with reluctance. Meanwhile, in the realm of so-called "peaceful trade" Japan traded with the communist countries. We now find that Tokyo's nonideological attitude toward trade and investment has placed it in a strong position to talk with Moscow and Peking about interesting and potentially important links. Rather than being competitive with a United States which has moved toward policies like those of Tokyo, Washington and Tokyo keep each other informed as to projects in which they may be involved jointly so as to improve the prospect of security of and enhance the economic gain from new ventures for all concerned.

Washington and Tokyo cooperate in the bilateral economic field in ways far too numerous to list here. How, actually, we cooperate has been obscured by the attention we devote to sore points in our relations with each other. The Japanese have helped the American farmer to make Japan by far the largest market for his output: we are selling almost $1.5 billion of agricultural produce to Japan every year. And now, after many years of resistance to American investors wishing to establish plants in Japan, there is emerging a dramatically different attitude toward such movements of capital between the two countries. All kinds of American investment are finding it easier to get into Japan. Meanwhile, Japan is seriously contemplating what will soon be seen to be a large flow of Japanese investment capital moving into the United States, creating jobs for American workers, and, incidentally, remedying in part present imbalances on payments account. As is so often the case with the Japanese, it will take some time for the benefits to us of this process to become fully apparent, and it is unlikely the Japanese will know quite how to take credit for the good they are doing.

In 1962 President Kennedy was responsible for launching a tradition of annual joint ministerial meetings on economic problems facing Japan and the United States. This is now but one example of literally scores of recurring meetings of Japanese and Americans who talk together, annually or more often, about security, economic, foreign policy planning, medical, environmental, cultural, scientific and other matters. Side by side with sessions involving government officials are other sessions involving private persons—business executives, economists and social scientists from our universities and think tanks, and so forth. Over the years there has been a continual increase in the candor of these encounters, and, on the Japanese side, a dramatic increase in linguistic competence and ease.

So, set against those matters to which the media in both countries pay attention as evidences of friction or worse, we should recall and seek improvement in the quality of the remakable and varied forms of our cooperation. To sum up specifically, our cooperation is intimate and creative in the fields of defense, trade, investment, foreign aid and cultural relations. We have reason to be proud of this relationship and what has come from it.

In conclusion, I would like to say a few words about the general notions of good luck, of responsibility and of opportunity.

Few people would deny, I suppose, that there was an element of good luck for the United States in the final outcome of World War II. The financial costs of that war were colossal. We had had ten million men under arms. We had suffered heavy casualties at sea, in the air and on the ground in both Europe and Asia. But our homeland was intact, and the fighting of the war had helped us to create for ourselves vast productive capacities. Our tradition of desiring to respond to simple human need—enshrined, prewar, in various institutional innovations to cope with the suffering of our Great Depression—together with our deep fear of communism as both an ideology and an apparatus of subversion, gave us motives for putting our productive capacities to work to assist in the recovery of our wartime friends and former enemies around the world. Two percent of our GNP went for a while into the Marshall Plan. To seize this postwar opportunity to assist in the rehabilitation of a weary and wounded world community proved to be what was needed to set in motion the dynamic of work, aspiration and self-discipline which ultimately brought into being the other two pillars of the industrialized Free World—Japan and the European Economic Community of today. American luck, opportunity and a sense of national responsibility combined to give the world much that was both good and bad in the bipolar and growth-oriented processes of international relations from 1945 to 1970.

In 1973 it is the United States which for a variety of reasons is crippled, notwithstanding the continuing growth of its $1 trillion GNP and its very high per capita income. Some might say that the war in Vietnam, and problems of race, of youth and of threats to environment, are causing a crisis of will and a sense of shrinking resources and fields for maneuver. The importance of the American economy to other countries around the world is something taken for granted. But both at home and abroad there are great doubts that this is a time when Washington can lead.

This is a moment, however, when it can be seen that Japan has cashed in on some extraordinarily lucky breaks. For the entire post–World War II period the charge on Japan's GNP for defense-security spending has been under 1 percent. 1948 legislation made possible a Japanese cutback of population growth to about 1 percent annually. For a century or more Japan has been dedicated to high quality mass education. And Japan enjoyed enormous foreign exchange gains from the fighting of wars in Korea and, subsequently, in Vietnam. The United States championed Japan's membership in the OECD and in the specialized agencies of the United Nations. Now, with its very great competitive advantages in the international monetary and commercial system, Japan has built up in excess of $18 billion in foreign exchange reserves. Japan has become in the words of some—"this nonpareil of a country."

Further, I perceive that Japan is fully conscious of the good luck in its recent past, it wishes to play a responsible role in the international community and it looks upon its opportunities as a chance to help both itself and its neighbors. I believe that the government of Japan spoke with utter sincerity in declaring its intention to devote 1 percent of its GNP to foreign aid by 1975. Already it has exceeded 0.9 percent. Thus, by 1975 it is very likely to exceed the expected $4 billion a year, and hopefully the present disappointing 0.23 percent in concessional aid will be much larger.

I see in Prime Minister Tanaka's plans for a remodeling of the home islands of Japan but one expression of a nationwide determination to improve the environment, diminish pollution and improve social welfare—and doing this will vastly increase Japan's need for trade balancing imports from countries all over the world.

I see in Japan's negotiations with Peking and with Moscow an intention to operate within a genuinely all-embracing world economy, and to do so on terms designed to break down barriers and reduce tensions. I see in the revaluation of the yen and the dramatic advances of liberalization on both current and capital account a determined Japanese effort to help in the strengthening of the dollar—this being motivated by recognition that continuing access to the American market is vital for the operation of the Japanese economic system.

Finally, let me suggest that in the decade to come Japan has the capacity, the intention and the will to improve upon the decision-making process needed to make Japan a primary shaping force for a new political economy in the Pacific area. This new system will accommodate many varying ideologies, will be committed to sustain growth, will strive to reduce disparities in wealth between the very rich and the very poor, and will reinforce global monetary and commercial arrangements intended to preserve economic equilibria and to lead to a general environment of confidence and safety for all peoples in the Pacific region.

Chapter Five

Comments

Allen B. Linden

These chapters stress the notion that Japan and the United States need one another. I heartily agree. I am concerned that the arguments over some economic issues, such as textiles, have been overstressed and have obscured healthy relations between our countries. It seems to me that Ambassador Sawaki has demonstrated that there are opportunities for American exports to Japan in two important areas: consumer goods and the technology to improve the quality of Japan's environment. The ambassador has also pointed out that one source of new relationships between Japan and the United States is the result of Japanese direct investment in our country.

There is an image of Japan in the United States which Mr. Barnett and Ambassador Sawaki hope will disappear, the image enbodied in the term "Japan, Incorporated." This term suggests that, somehow or other, Japan is a tightly organized coalition of bankers, government leaders and businessmen with whom it is impossible for American firms to compete.

A column written by Henry C. Wallich in *Newsweek,* April 16, 1973, shows the influence of the image of "Japan, Incorporated." Wallich opens his column with the suggestion that the average Japanese may enjoy a higher per capita income than the average American by the 1980s. He asks, rhetorically, "How is Japan doing it?" In part, according to Wallich, the answer lies in the character of the Japanese people, who have the habit of saving and investing a high proportion of their income.

Mr. Wallich continues:

> Particularly striking is the way in which Japan has ignored the precepts of Western economics and finance. The U.S. believes in free unrestricted competition. Japan, without ignoring competition, believes in cooperation. The U.S. believes in free markets. Japan believes in keeping things under control.

Wallich states that Japanese firms, banks and government agencies cooperate to keep large firms from failing. He comments: "In Japan nobody would question that a large and important firm like Lockheed should be saved." Because of governmental and financial support, Wallich contends that large Japanese firms are able to take risks which American firms cannot consider.

Wallich concludes that the United States cannot follow Japan's example in seeking economic growth. He states: "I doubt that the U.S. could benefit from the example of Japan, even if it knew how to follow it. We are an open society, anti-authoritarian, and whatever successes we may have must be rooted in those characteristics. We may admire the Japanese performance, but we cannot imitate it."

Here is a rather sophisticated presentation of the image of "Japan, Incorporated." Japan is seen as a closed, authoritarian society in which a coalition of governmental, financial and business leaders work together to pursue national goals even if that means maintaining inefficient firms. This image is a major obstacle to relations between the United States and Japan.

Is this image valid? A group of American and Japanese specialists in the study of the Japanese economy and society do not think so.

At a conference on Japanese organization and decision making held in Hawaii in January 1973, scholars of our two countries came to conclusions quite different from those of Henry C. Wallich. In a report on the conference, Professor Ezra Vogel, Director of the East Asian Research Center, Harvard University, commented on the notion of "Japan, Incorporated":

> Relations between government and business tend to be closer in Japan than in the United States. However, to say that Japanese government and business together behave like a single corporation, a notion which has taken on pernicious overtones amid American businessmen's displeasure over Japanese competition, vastly distorts the structure and overstates the strength of this relationship. It is true that government, in general, does take a more active role in supporting programs in the interest of Japanese business as a whole, but empirical evidence concerning the frequency of cabinet-level contacts with businessmen, the extent to which Diet members represent business interests, the willingness of firms to follow governmental guidance, and the extent to which government involves itself in business decisions simply does not begin to sustain the "Japan, Incorporated" proposition. Indeed there is considerable doubt whether the business circles make up a coherent enough entity to adequately represent Japanese business interests before government.

To American and Japanese scholars Japan is a complex society in which there are competing interests; businessmen are not all of one mind and there is frustration and conflict in the relationship between the business community and the government.

Which view of Japan—"Japan, Incorporated" or complex, competitive Japan—will prevail in American public opinion? In the concern over the protection of American business interests today, I fear that the calm, rational statement of the academicians will be neglected and the image of "Japan, Incorporated" will be stressed.

For this reason, I am less optimistic about the future of relations between the United States and Japan than either Ambassador Sawaki or Mr. Barnett. I think that relations between our two countries can grow worse rather than better in the 1970s.

Mr. Barnett has pointed out that the mid–1970s will be a period of declining opportunities and sluggishness in the economic growth of the United States. There will be a tendency to blame Japan for our supposed economic misfortunes. After all, when one sees on television twelve Japanese couples honeymooning at Elsinore castle because it is cheaper to have a wedding in Denmark than in Japan, one wonders about Japanese wealth. The notion of the riches of Japan is further fed by stories in the *New York Times* about the purchases by Japanese of all sorts of art. The image of rich Japan is counterpointed by stories of economic hardship in the United States, such as the projection in the American press that, if prices continue to rise, an American middle class family would not be able to buy a home of its own, ever.

I have been talking about images of Japanese wealth and American hardship. Ambassador Sawaki has presented us with some of the facts which can dispel these images. The images, however, will persist.

There is another area of concern which leads me to be more gloomy than Ambassador Sawaki and Mr. Barnett about the future of U.S.–Japanese relations; that is the new international political situation in the world. Japan, the United States, the Soviet Union and the People's Republic of China are in the process of redefining their relationships with one another. One cannot expect relations between the United States and Japan to continue as they were in the past. If for no other reason than the "Nixon shocks," which have already been mentioned, I think that the Japanese would be foolish not to reconsider their relationships with the United States. It would be idiotic to put all one's eggs in a Republican basket where an elephant might sit upon them.

I would like Ambassador Sawaki and Mr. Barnett to consider four questions which I feel deal with issues that might generate misunderstanding and conflict between the United States and Japan.

First, is there growing competition between the United States and Japan for shares of the China market; We both offer the sorts of goods that the People's Republic is seeking, products of a high order of technology. Until President Nixon's initiative, Japan supplied more to China than any other country. Is there a potential for tension between us over shares of the market there?

A second question is one which was raised by Mr. Barnett: Will there be an official role for Japan in the rehabilitation of Laos, Cambodia and

Vietnam? Mr. Sawaki omitted these regions in his listing of the regions to which Japan is sending foreign aid. We know, however, that there is much Japanese private investment in those areas. Does Japan plan to play a role in the rehabilitation of those war-torn countries?

Thirdly, is it possible in the present confusion in international relations for Japan to avoid building up its military strength? Is it not necessary for Japan, in its quest for security amidst the powers, to rearm?

Finally, what is going to be done about the unresolved status of Taiwan? Is it possible that the issue of Taiwan could become a significant irritant in the relations between the United States and Japan?

I have raised these four questions to suggest some of the problems that face Japan and the United States in the next ten years.

Part II

Enduring Perspectives of Pacific
Power Plays: Historical Aspects

Chapter Six

Introduction

Frank D. McCann

Americans often seem to view the Pacific Basin as a vast lake shared by themselves and the Japanese. If, for a moment, images of sea power and economic strength are put aside, a glance at the globe will reveal more than two dozen countries washed by Pacific waters. Canada, Mexico, Peru, Chile, Australia, the Philippines, the Soviet Union and, of course China should be taken into account when one considers the future of the basin. The regionalist approach to international studies can be detrimental to developing a clear picture of so vast a portion of the world, unless, as each segment is studied, it is related to other segments.

The two chapters in this section, by the diplomatic historians Akira Iriye and Eugene P. Trani, examine relations between the Pacific's major powers, focusing on their unfortunate 1941–1945 war and, implicitly, on the possibility of future conflict. This binational emphasis is justified in that the destinies of the basin's nations will be effected for good or ill by the quality of the relations between the two major powers. If they pursue a course of cooperation, the other nations will find themselves being drawn into trade and investment relationships which will either lead to mercantile interdependence or to some new form of independent development, perhaps along lines such as are occurring in Peru. If their course is strewn with conflict, the basin's nations will be forced into alliance systems as each side scrambles for natural resources. At any rate, no Pacific nation will go unaffected whatever the major powers' course.

United States interest in the Pacific has been based on economics—the desire for markets and routes to them, or for natural resources. The strategic elements in United States policy exist to protect the national economy and the far-flung connections. Historically, the nation's involvements in the Pacific resulted from Thomas Jefferson's 1803 purchase of Louisiana Territory from Napoleon. That, in due course, produced nearly a century of warfare with

dozens of Indian nations, the invasion and conquest of Mexico, the incorporation of half of that country into the United States, the purchase of Alaska to
fend off the Russians, the engineering of a coup d'état in Hawaii, an unnecessary
war with Spain, the bloody supression of the Philippine independence movement, the taking of Panama, and numerous armed interventions in the Caribbean
and Central America to protect the route to the Pacific. Against that backdrop,
the so-called Open Door Notes were announcements to the world that the
United States wanted to play in the China game, preferably according to its own
rules. Such a desire, not surprisingly, led to conflict with Japan, which regarded
China, much as the United States regarded Mexico, as its special sphere to be
exploited at will.

The role of perceptions in the formation and execution of foreign
policy is especially important when potential adversaries or allies do not know
each other intimately. Given the Americans' obvious willingness to use force in
dealing with nonwhite peoples, the Japanese surmised in 1941 that a pre-emptive
strike was necessary to blunt the attack they believed would come. But I suspect
that the Japanese did not have a clear notion of how Americans perceived them.
They were, in American eyes, the Europeans of Asia, whom they respected. The
American tendency throughout the nineteenth century was to avoid war with
respected peoples. It is doubtful that the United States would have fought the
Japanese over China alone. The irony, of course, is that while the Japanese and
the Americans fought, the Chinese seized control of their own territory. The
Pacific war was a gigantic exercise for foolhardiness and futility.

If Japan's policy objectives in the 1930s were raw materials and
markets and its policy means were its armies and navy, then it appears in the
1970s that only its policy means have changed. If it was competition for China's
resources and markets that led to war in 1941, then it is safe to assume that the
current Japanese–American competition in Latin America, Southeast Asia and
perhaps one day again in China will inevitably produce a clash in the future. But
while it is equally safe to assume that the clash will not be an armed one, its
nature and results cannot be easily determined.

Americans should learn an important lesson from World War II.
While they concentrated on their competitor, the prize they were struggling for
escaped. In recent years the United States press and academic community
seemed locked into the wartime mind-set of viewing American–Japanese relations as a one-to-one situation, largely ignoring the locales where they were
competing. Moreover, while we have restricted ourselves in these essays to the
Pacific Basin, it might well be that a regional or geographic focus for any
purpose other than analytical examination is outmoded. Certainly, United States
policies must be based on global, as well as regional, considerations.

Japanese and American interests are now competing heavily in Latin
America—in an area the Americans thought of as their preserve. And Americans
are often responsible for the competitive situation because they failed to invest

properly, to market goods imaginatively and to analyze market potential. Indeed, they helped create Japanese competition in the early sixties by withdrawing investment dollars from Latin America and placing them in Japan, thereby either creating or freeing Japanese money for investment in Latin American countries. By studying the market and by helping it to grow, the Japanese have been able to infiltrate important sectors of the national economies. It is simply not sufficient to maintain a bilateral emphasis when much of the interaction is taking place elsewhere. While the Japanese–American war was produced by competition over a third party, I would hope that in the future the two countries would find ways to cooperate in their dealings with others. Of course, my hope assumes a certain community of interest, which may or may not actually exist. But by analyzing their bilateral relations against the background of regions or countries in which they are competing, perhaps common interests and areas of cooperation can be determined.

Chapter Seven

Four American Fiddlers and Their Far Eastern Tunes: A Survey of Japanese–American Relations, 1898–1941

Eugene P. Trani

Any survey of Japanese–American relations between 1898 and 1941 must be just that—a survey. The subject is too broad, too complex, too significant to lend itself to a neat thirty-page package.[1] Many issues crowd the interaction between the two major non-European powers that came to maturity during that period. Territorial acquisitions, immigration, the power balance in Asia, naval rivalry, China, economic competition and other issues—all stand in the way of generalization about the period.

Yet some comments can be made. The forty-three years from 1898 to 1941 can be discussed in a variety of ways, and one of the most interesting and important is to go beyond the events of interaction, whether formal diplomacy or informal contact, and look to the roles of the United States and Japan. How did the United States view Japan? What role did the United States see for itself in the Pacific and what role for Japan? Did these roles change? These questions, of course, introduce others. What about the Japanese and their roles? But emphasis here will be on the United States and the roles it defined, as expressed by four major American statesmen of the period.

To approach this topic in terms of roles poses difficulties. The distinction between government and people is perhaps most obvious. Sometimes government leaders hold certain beliefs about American behavior in East Asia with which the people, or at least some of them, disagree. There have been disputes within the government, between the president and officials in the State Department, the Departments of the Navy and Army and other agencies, about the Far East. And events sometimes outrun plans, and a course of action can take place irrespective of and even in opposition to the roles a government has set up. Yet between 1898 and 1941 there were generally accepted views in America of the roles for the United States and Japan. It is to these roles that this essay is directed.

The period of increasing conflict of the United States and Japan, between 1898 and 1941, breaks into four divisions, each approximately a decade long and each with different American roles.[2] In each division a major figure stands out as spokesman for the role of the moment. The first division, from 1898 to 1909, was dominated by Theodore Roosevelt. The United States looked at Japan with a mixture of admiration and suspicion. Here the tune Roosevelt played for Japanese listeners was "Expend to the Mainland." The second division was from 1909 to 1920. In that decade the United States viewed Japan as a modern imperial power. It changed the role it perceived for itself, and that it perceived for Japan, with a growing belief in the need to help China, which country it saw as the hope of the future in East Asia. The significance of that eleven year period in Japanese–American relations is only now beginning to be understood. The tune of the decade, played most frequently by President Woodrow Wilson, was "Imperialism Is Over." The third division, from 1920 to 1931, was a period of calm in relations as each country changed to peacetime economies, concentrated on economics and worked to consolidate the gains of World War I. The United States accepted Japan as a major power in the Pacific. Here the tune was "International Cooperation," and the principal musician was Charles Evans Hughes. The last division, from 1931 to 1941, has often been referred to as a decade of hostility, and Japan appeared an aggressor nation. While war was perhaps not inevitable, any "significant disposition toward peaceful solutions was strikingly absent from this decade."[3] The American tune of the decade, played by Henry L. Stimson, was "Stop the Aggression." What is most interesting about these different American tunes and the roles they ascribed is that the Japanese, after much difficulty and with many reservations, danced to the first three tunes, but decided to play their own in the 1930s.

Some specific comments about each division and its spokesman are in order. By the end of 1898 the United States and Japan stood as powers not merely with major interests in East Asia but with major points of disagreement. Their relations up until that year had been generally good. It was the United States, through Commodore Matthew C. Perry, that opened Japan in 1853. Interchanges for the next thirty-five years were cordial as Japan worked to build up strength to protect itself from the West. As Japan modernized, trade with the United States benefited both countries. Americans went to Japan to preach technology, Christianity and democracy, while Japanese came to the United States to trade and study. The United States Naval Academy's graduating class of 1881 symbolized the spirit of Japanese–American relations in the last half of the nineteenth century. Among the three Japanese graduates was Uryu Soto-kichi, later one of the naval heroes of the Russo–Japanese War. The American graduates included John W. Weeks, later senator from Massachusetts and Warren G. Harding's secretary of war, and Ovington E. Weller, who was to serve as senator from Maryland.[4] Americans looked with admiration as the Japanese quickly mastered much Western technology, treated American visitors with kindness and adopted a more democratic form of government. There were moments of controversy and issues of contention, but generally Japan was viewed as a country that was progressive and increasingly democratic, following in the footsteps of the United States.

Feeling began to change at the end of the century, particularly with the successful conclusion of wars by each nation—the Sino–Japanese War which ended in 1895, and the Spanish–American War of 1898. Before that time the interests of the United States in East Asia were limited. Trade was important, and there were missionaries in much of Asia. America had territorial outposts in or touching the Pacific: California, Alaska, an interest in Samoa. But Washington had no real Far Eastern policy. With the 1898 annexation of Hawaii, and the acquisition of Guam and the Philippines as a result of the Spanish–American War, the government was forced to think seriously about the Far East. Japan, fresh from a smashing victory over China, loomed large on the diplomatic horizon. The Sino–Japanese and Spanish–American Wars marked the real emergence of the victors as expansionist powers in East Asia.[5] From that point on, a collision of the interests of the United States and Japan, though not necessarily in war, was nearly inevitable.

Events of the years from 1898 to 1909, so important in Japanese–American relations, can best be understood by following the reaction of one American, Theodore Roosevelt. While the majority of Americans thought little about contacts with Japan, TR was representative of many who did. He was an expansionist and supported the American movement into world affairs as the nineteenth century came to a close. For a variety of reasons, he believed expansion necessary for the advancement of the United States, with benefits resulting for the rest of the world. He viewed world affairs in strategic relations and felt a keen affinity for Great Britain. During his prepresidential years he called for the annexation of Hawaii, served in the war against Spain, favored keeping Guam and the Philippines, supported the Open Door Notes and argued the case for a large navy.

As the twentieth century began, and Britain was in obvious decline as a world power, Roosevelt believed the United States had a large role in the Far Eastern picture and sought to define the position of both the United States and Japan in East Asia. Throughout his public life he was torn between admiration for Japanese efficiency and fighting qualities and concern about their military strength. While he had expressed irritation at Japan's protest against possible American annexation of Hawaii in 1897 and had worried about the Philippine Islands after 1898, by the time he became president in 1901 admiration had overcome fear. He supported Japan's new position of prominence in East Asia. He decided that Japan did not threaten important American interests. He saw the Japanese as a barrier to Russian expansion, as a preserver of the balance of power in East Asia, as a protector of the open door and as a potential stabilizer of China, a nation for which he had little respect. He supported the

Anglo–Japanese alliance, concluded in 1902. He understood the necessity of avoiding war to protect American East Asian interests, especially on the Chinese mainland. The American people simply would not support such a war, and TR thought with good reason, as even the successful conclusion of such a war would not guarantee American interests there.[6]

Roosevelt had set up roles for the United States and Japan. While the American government had commercial and naval interests in the Far East, it had limited power. Japanese interests, especially on the mainland, seemed not to conflict with those of the United States. While Japan and the United States were potential naval and commercial rivals, they should work together. It was with that view that Roosevelt supported Japan in its war with Russia in 1904–1905 which ended with a peace treaty signed at the Portsmouth Navy Yard.[7] To be sure, Roosevelt was aware of the possibility of Japan's getting "puffed with pride," should the Japanese decisively defeat the Russians. He hoped that Japan, if victorious, would not threaten American interests in China. But he recognized that Japan would have special interests on the Asian mainland, and supported the Japanese claim to Korea. At one point he even talked about a Japanese Monroe Doctrine in the Far East. TR hoped to arrange a balanced antagonism between Russia and Japan after the war.

That outcome proved impossible. Japan's defeat of Russia was so decisive and other events intervening in Japanese–American relations so important that TR had a change of heart as to the Japanese role in East Asia. At that point he began to play for the Japanese a special tune, "Expand to the Mainland." After 1905, Japan moved to close the door in Manchuria and the Sino–Japanese rivalry intensified. Roosevelt's mind was elsewhere. Not only were there problems in Europe, but even in the Far East the whole relationship between the United States and Japan changed, at least in his mind. He became more concerned about possessions in the Far East, referring to the Philippines in 1907 as the United States's "heel of Achilles," and became alarmed over an immigration crisis between the two countries.[8] He saw that Japan could expand either to the west or east, and hoped to trade off an increased Japanese presence in China for guarantees of the security of American possessions in the Pacific and a solution to the immigration crisis. The period from 1905 to 1909 was difficult for him, given Japanese disappointment over the Portsmouth peace, the continuing immigration issue, a real war scare and naval expansion. There was continued Japanese expansion in East Asia but TR saw such a course as natural.

The most important part about the president's view of the new situation was his belief that the open door in China was not worth war with Japan. He believed that the United States should do what it could to preserve its interests in China, but that it should recognize Japan as the dominant power on the Asian mainland. In short, he gave a green light to Japanese expansion in Manchuria. One of the best expressions of this belief appeared in a letter to Secretary of State-designate Philander C. Knox on February 8, 1909, shortly before leaving office.[9] He noted that Japanese–American relations were of "great and permanent importance." While Japanese immigration to the United States had to stop, the Washington government should "show all possible courtesy and consideration." The Taft administration had to understand that "Japan is vitally interested in China and on the Asiatic mainland and her wiser statesmen will if possible prevent her getting entangled in a war with us, because whatever its result it would hamper and possibly ruin Japan when she came to deal again with affairs in China." Since the Pacific Coast of the United States was defenseless and "we have no army to hold or reconquer the Philippines and Hawaii," the United States had to avoid war. TR felt that China and American interests in that country were insignificant in the broader context of America's Far Eastern policy. Consider how different things might have been, had such a philosophy been at work during the 1930s.

It is interesting that the Japanese, after long discussion and with reluctance for they wanted to combine peaceful economic expansion to the east with a new presence in China, decided in 1908 to dance to TR's tune and concentrate on continental expansion. They felt that this was a course that would avoid conflict with the United States—something which had become a concern of military planners in the United States.[10]

The years from 1898 to 1909 saw initial controversy in Japanese–American relations. 1898 had begun with the United States a minor power in East Asia, with little involvement in that area. By 1909 all that had changed. Russia was nearly gone from the East Asia equation, smashed by Japan. Britain, France and Germany maintained interests in the Far East, but as the years marched on to 1914 and the grand collision in Europe, these nations took less interest in Asia. Japan and the United States remained and by 1909 both had large stakes in the Far East. During the years from 1898 to 1909 all the major issues of Japanese–American relations came to the fore. Trade, expansion, naval rivalry, immigration had all become obvious. But there was no war. The American government, and especially Roosevelt, recognized that Japan had legitimate interests in the Far East and prepared to allow Japan a major role. There was suspicion, but there was also respect and even admiration, as Americans looked to Japan.

My distinguished colleague, Akira Iriye, has suggested that the years after 1906 mark the beginning of estrangement—political, diplomatic, ideological and even psychological—of the Americans and the Japanese. This is true. But the estrangement became pronounced and in the long run more significant when the United States, in addition to other rivalries with Japan, began to oppose Japanese continental expansion.[11] That did not happen until Roosevelt left the White House. The Japanese then discovered that Roosevelt's green light in China had changed to red, and was to remain so for most of the time until 1941.

The years from 1909 to 1920 were decisive for relations between Japan and America. Events that worsened that relationship crowded those years.

American efforts to restore the open door in Manchuria, the continuing immigration crisis, naval expansion, American sympathy for the Chinese Revolution, Washington's reaction to the Twenty-One Demands and the Shantung settlement, Japanese–American contention at Paris, intervention in Siberia, and growth of antagonistic caricatures in many minds within each country of the other, all these made the eleven year period, at least in my estimation, perhaps the most important decade in relations between these countries prior to 1941. Relations in 1909 mixed suspicion with respect, but by 1920 had undergone such tension that Japan, in the minds of many Americans, had become the expected antagonist in East Asia. The same process was occurring in Japan.

While Woodrow Wilson was the dominant American figure in Japanese–American relations during that period, some comments about the years between TR and Wilson are necessary. Even as the Roosevelt administration came to an end, forces were at work which would reverse TR's policy and change the roles that America saw in East Asia. After 1905, as Roosevelt turned attention elsewhere, the State Department regained control of diplomacy toward East Asia. In 1908, Elihu Root established the department's first geographic unit, the Division of Far Eastern Affairs. The new structure provided "an opportunity for policy to move upward from lower bureaucratic levels."[12] While not significant in the last year of TR's administration, the division even then opposed Japanese expansion into China. Opposition to Japan's China policy eventually dominated the division and became a most important factor in the years from 1909 to 1941.

With urging from the bureaucracy and because of a combination of economic and moral motives, the Taft administration changed policy toward East Asia. Power balances became less important. An ability and even willingness to consider specific problems as parts of larger pictures became rarer. The Taft administration was less interested in Europe, and it increased American involvement in Latin America and China. For Japanese–American relations the latter shift had importance. Encouraged by State Department officials like Francis M. Huntington Wilson and Willard Straight, the Taft administration decided to challenge Japan's newly established preeminence in Manchuria. The Open Door Notes, which had changed in meaning after 1900, assumed importance in Japanese–American relations. The reasons for the change in American policy were complicated. There was a need for economic expansion, the growing suspicion of and resentment against Japan, and, most important, a faith in the future and importance of China. In the long run the effort to loosen Japan's grip on Manchuria failed mightily.

Faith in China increased during the Wilson years as the tension rose between Washington and Tokyo. Japan became a rival in China, as well as a military and commercial threat in the Pacific. Wilson approached foreign policy from a different framework than Theodore Roosevelt. He did not look at foreign policy in terms of balance but rather envisioned a new era in which foreign affairs would move from imperialism to a new community of interest. In earlier years Wilson had supported the Spanish–American War and acquisition of territory in the Pacific. In his *History of the American People,* published in 1902, he wrote that the United States "could not easily have dispensed with that foothold in the East which the possession of the Philippines so unexpectedly afforded them." Still, he favored preparation of the Philippines for self-government. In a lecture at Waterbury, Connecticut in December 1900, he warned the American people not to expect the Philippines to adopt "an American form of government."[13] He thought territorial conquest was part of the foreign policy of the past, and from 1913 onward, but especially with the controversy over the Twenty-One Demands, began to play his tune of "Imperialism Is Over" for the Japanese.

When he entered office he was not anti-Japanese, but he was certainly pro-Chinese. Many writers have made the point that Wilson never exhibited to the Japanese the "same sympathy and tolerance with which he viewed and treated China. Standards of international morality which he held so highly were often waived in judging China but applied rigidly and without insight in dealing with Japan."[14] There are several explanations for this. Wilson judged Japan to be an advanced nation and accountable for its behavior. As early as 1889, the then young professor at Wesleyan University in Connecticut had commented upon Japan's maturity. He had pointed out the similarities between the constitutions of Prussia and Japan and noted: "And I think that, considering the stage of development in which Japan now finds herself, the Prussian constitution was an excellent instrument to copy. Her choice of it as a model is but another proof of the singular sagacity, the singular power to see and learn, which is Japan's best constitution and promise of success."[15] It was perhaps significant that he saw Japan moving in the footsteps of Prussia. It was not so much that Wilson viewed Japan as an Asian nation but as a modern nation, and he became critical of its expansionist tendencies.

Wilson had warm feelings for China. Because of his acquaintance with missionaries, his connection with China through Princeton and his own thinking, he had great sympathy for China, mixed with a sense of superiority. He had supported Chinese exclusion, writing that American laborers could not compete with the "thrifty, skilful" Chinese, but condemned the wanton attacks upon Chinese in America. He reacted positively to the Chinese Revolution, seeing the long-suppressed Chinese as a people beginning to come into their own.[16] In the main his Far Eastern policy concerned China, and China became the dominant factor in Japanese–American relations. He indicated his pro–Chinese policy by three moves early in his administration: he withdrew support for a Chinese consortium, believing it an effort to continue imperialism in China; he recognized the government of Yuan Shih-k'ai, hoping Yuan would bring stability; and he took great care in naming his minister to China, a place where "the interests of China and of the Christian world are so intimately involved."[17]

China, to Wilson, had become a nation under siege by imperialist nations, of which Japan was one of the most important. For him, the United States had a mission: to help the Chinese on their path to participation in world affairs.

These considerations led to a change in the American roles for Japan and the United States. The United States added to its role assistance to China to oppose the imperialist nations. This meant a shift in the role for Japan. While Wilson and Americans in general still recognized Japan's large interests on the Asian mainland, gone was the feeling that these interests could operate to the exclusion of Americans and to the injury of Chinese. The years of campaigning by missionaries, merchants interested in the China market and philosophers of democracy who pictured the Chinese as ready to adopt that form of government and follow in the footsteps of the United States, were beginning to pay off.

Japanese conduct during the World War increased Wilson's pro–Chinese feelings, and by mid–1915 had made him anti-Japanese. The World War had profound repercussions for Japanese–American relations. By the end of the war, the United States looked to the Pacific with greater concern than the Atlantic. The Japanese had seen the war in Europe as a great opportunity. William L. Neumann has written that "capable and ambitious leaders had learned that the code of international politics permitted one nation's troubles to be another nation's gain."[18]

Dissatisfied with peaceful continentalism on the Asian mainland, blocked by the United States from eastward expansion, Japanese officials in 1914 decided to seize the German concessions in China and in the Pacific north of the equator. The controversy over the Twenty-One Demands which followed shortly was highly important in Japanese–American relations, for "from this point onward American support of China's territorial and administrative integrity has been seen as a prime source of tension." Wilson was unwilling to intervene militarily in this controversy, but American diplomatic policy opposed Japan. The United States would not recognize any impairment of what was "commonly known as the open door policy." Burton Beers believes that the United States missed an opportunity, recognized by Robert Lansing, to resolve general Japanese–American problems, but given Wilson's beliefs toward the roles of the United States and Japan in East Asia it is hard to imagine how the differences could have been resolved.[19]

In the summer of 1915 the president's attention left the Far East, turning to Europe and his ensuing bid for re-election. The submarine crisis, the Russian Revolution of 1917, entry into the war and eventually the terms of peace, all consumed the president's time and interest. Asia in the years after 1915 became a secondary consideration. Only in Paris in 1919 did it become a major problem. It is true that the Lansing–Ishii agreements of 1917 reduced some of the tension between the United States and Japan, especially concerning Chinese commerce, but problems remained. Beers properly views this agreement as "a symbol of the triumph of presidential idealism over Secretary Lansing's desire for a realistic Japanese–American accord."[20] And there was the Siberian intervention which certainly heightened tension between the two countries, with American mistrust of Japanese intentions in Russia.

But at Paris the East Asian problem exploded.[21] The Japanese pressed for German rights in Shantung, a paramount position in Eastern Asia, acceptance of wartime treaties with China, a declaration of racial equality and control of German islands in the North Pacific. The Japanese failed to get the statement on equality and gained only mandate control, through the League of Nations, of some of the German islands. The big stake was Shantung and a general solution of the Chinese problem. Wilson's advisers called for return to China of German rights in Shantung, but the Japanese insisted on retaining them. After difficult negotiations, complicated by prior treaties between Japan and France and Great Britain, and a Japanese threat to boycott the treaty and the league, the Japanese won control of German economic rights in Shantung. Wilson opposed the claims, but saw the solution as a compromise—one final bit of imperialism in hope that the league would bring a new order. His feelings about the compromise were revealed in a letter sent to an American missionary who served in China, the Reverend Dr. Samuel I. Woodbridge, who had married Wilson's first cousin, Jeanie Woodrow. A frequent correspondent about Chinese matters, Woodbridge criticized the compromise. Obviously stung, Wilson replied:

> France and Great Britain absolutely bound themselves by treaty to Japan with regard to the Shantung Settlement as it stands in the Treaty with Germany. What would you propose that we should do? To refuse to concur in the Treaty with Germany would not alter the situation in China's favor, unless it is your idea that we should force Great Britain and France to break their special treaty with Japan, and how would you suggest that we should do that? By the exercise of what sort of force?

> Japan, as you know, has promised to retain much less than the terms of the treaty give her. She has consented to bind herself by all the engagements of the Covenant of the League of Nations, and if the United States is to be a party to this treaty and a member of the League, she will have an opportunity for serving China in all matters of international justice such as she has never had before, and such as she could not obtain by the course you suggest.[22]

This ended Wilson's policy toward Japan. Had the president been interested in changing the Shantung arrangement, the opportunity passed. In the early autumn of 1919 Wilson left on his "swing around the circle," curtailed when he became ill. He returned to Washington only to suffer a thrombosis, paralyzing his left side and virtually all of his future presidential activity. Foreign affairs suffered because of lack of leadership. John V. A. MacMurray, chief of the Far Eastern Division of the State Department, wrote that Wilson "has been so exclusively responsible for policies—particularly in the realm of foreign affairs—the whole administration has been so much of a one man show—that his disability has paralyzed the whole executive. One has that queer feeling of a ship at sea with engines stopped."[23]

The Japanese eventually came to accept Wilson's tune of "Imperialism Is Over" and retreated somewhat from Shantung to develop their other territories. That was too late for Wilson and many Americans. It is hard to overestimate the importance of the decade from 1909 to 1920 in Japanese–American relations. By the latter year the whole Far Eastern balance had changed. What remaining Russian power there was in this area after 1905 had disappeared with the revolutions of 1917 not to return until the mid–1920s. Defeat by the Allies had removed Germany from Asia. European concerns during this period overshadowed France's limited interest there. Three powers remained: Britain, Japan, the United States. Compared to their worldwide interests, the Far East was not as significant to the British as to the Japanese and Americans. Between these latter two powers the contrast was great. The Japanese seemed to stand for the old diplomacy of imperialism, the Americans (at least in their own minds) for the new diplomacy of international cooperation. The contrast had turned the fear and respect with which the United States viewed Tokyo to a deep-seated suspicion mixed with resentment. China had become the major Far Eastern concern of Americans. The Japanese could no longer expect to get rights in China denied in the Eastern Pacific. The moral adoption of China was decisive, the major change in Japanese–American relations between 1909 and 1920.

As the Wilson administration came to a close, it was apparent to both Americans and Japanese that some attempt had to be made to bring a reconsideration of the relations between the two countries. That attempt was symbolized by the Washington Naval Conference, where the leading American diplomat playing the tune of "International Cooperation" was Charles Evans Hughes.

Hughes had had little background in foreign affairs before taking control of the Department of State in 1921. His formal training consisted of teaching a course on international law during two years at the Cornell University Law School in the early 1890s. But by 1921 he had adopted some views on foreign policy. He seemed to stand in contrast to Wilson by noting that "foreign policies are not built upon abstractions" but resulted from international cooperation which recognized "divergent national ambitions." He believed that war was a continuing feature of international relations and thought the most important task of the diplomat was to avoid war. Hughes held little hope for the repression of armed conflict by radical revision of international law. He saw no point—and here his disagreement with Wilson was a clear—in advocating formulas "which may legally require a state to act against its vital interests." This led him to the "most distinctive" enterprise of his times—"the development of institu-

tions for the promotion of international arbitration, adjudication, and concilia-
tion, as well as the codification of traditional international law."[24] He stressed
international law and diplomatic accommodation, while recognizing the existence of power. Hughes believed in progressive development of world order,
but realized that development would be slow and that attempts at radical change
were bound to fail.

What did all of this mean for Japanese–American relations? Hughes
sensed that China had to be placed in the broader context of United States East
Asian policy, but was also part of Japanese–American relations. He was willing
to draw back from the Wilson position which had isolated China as a consideration of foreign policy. Hughes lacked any exaggerated sentiment for China and
believed that conditions of peace and economic interdependence would dominate in the 1920s, and for the Far East this meant a need for order and stability.[25] America and Japan had to promote interests and reconcile differences.
The controversies of 1909–1920—immigration, naval rivalry, trade, territorial
issues, China—had become too intense.

Hughes attempted this broad resettlement in Japanese–American
relations at the Washington Conference and played his tune of "International
Cooperation" with vigor. The conference and related agreements stand as the
most thorough consideration of the Far Eastern problems that occurred between
the United States and Japan before 1941. The agreements of Washington are
familiar, only the highpoints need mention. The United States acknowledged
Japan's wartime gains in the Pacific in the Four-Power Treaty. The Nine-Power
Treaty dealt with China. While Hughes supported Chinese territorial and
administrative integrity, he "undertook no major assault upon those long-
standing restrictions on Chinese sovereignty associated with extraterritorial
rights and international control of the Chinese tariff."[26] Hughes did seek to gain
Japan's retreat from Shantung. Shantung lay outside the proceedings of the
conference, but Hughes saw the Japanese ambassador and Chinese minister and
persuaded their countries to negotiate the issue by themselves during the
conference. He took part in the talks, exerting pressure to bring a settlement and
even holding the final meeting at his house. A treaty between Japan and China
on Shantung was signed February 4, 1922. Hughes did not gain a Japanese
retreat from Manchuria. They were too entrenched. But the Japanese did make
concessions, withdrawing some of the harshest of the Twenty-One Demands.
They also agreed to evacuate Siberia and northern Sakhalin. "Behind the verbal
cover of the Washington arrangements, however, there was an actual accommodation to the recent acquisitions of Japan in the Pacific and China and an
attempt to secure that new status through international pledge."[27] The Four-
Power Treaty called only for consultation by the signatories and the Nine-Power
Treaty had no enforcement provisions in it.

In some ways the most original part of the Washington Conference
was the attempt to solve naval differences, which by 1920 had become a central

concern in Japanese–America relations. It was an effort to avoid an arms race, and was based on the maintenance of the military status quo. To be sure the Five-Power Treaty dealt only with capital ships, but Hughes hoped this would be a significant beginning, especially when combined with the nonfortification provisions of that treaty. Certainly this agreement was a recognition by the United States of Japanese naval importance in the Pacific.[28]

Hughes believed that the Washington Conference was a beginning. He saw all the agreements—the Four-, Five- and Nine-Power Treaties, the Sino–Japanese Treaty on Shantung, the Japanese–American agreement settling the controversy over the island of Yap, the Japanese promise to withdraw from Siberia and the later abrogation of the Lansing–Ishii Agreement—with their political, economic and military terms, as significant departures from the increased tension that had grown between Japan and the United States. The picture that eventually emerged from the Washington initiative was the result of "a procession of gigantic horse trades in which each power sought to buy maximum security at minimum expense. Concessions in one treaty were paid for in others, until the complex process of give and take had been completed."[29] Hughes hoped that the nations would add self-restraint and good will on top of the agreements and that all would then contribute to a sense of security. He did think that the conference had discovered specific formulas which harmonized the interests of the participating nations.

This approach was a departure from the Wilson view, more realistic in dealing with Japanese–American relations, even if the conference was full of weakness and if powers remained unsatisfied. Two of the countries that held large stakes in East Asia before 1914—Germany and Russia—were not represented. The absence of Russia was most significant, for in the 1920s the new Soviet government pursued its own policy and did all it could to bring the expulsion of the United States, Japan and Britain from positions of dominance on the Asian mainland. China was also slighted, remaining an object of American, Japanese and British diplomacy, not an equal participant in that diplomacy. And just as certainly the United States was again asking Japan to change its role in East Asia and to accommodate its foreign policy to another western model— from imperialism to international cooperation, particularly economic cooperation. The Japanese government approved the Washington system, but as Professor Iriye has so clearly shown in his book *After Imperialism: The Search for a New Order in the Far East, 1921–1931,* the Japanese "army and navy supreme headquarters had continued to regard conflict with the United States as likely and made this the basic assumption in their defense policies."[30] Such developments were not limited to Japanese planners. American strategists revised their Orange Plan in 1924. While civil leaders in both countries continued to stress international cooperation, military planners prepared for war. In the end, at least in Japan, this separation of military policy from foreign policy had great significance.

With completion of the Washington system, Hughes turned attention to other areas of policy, and in the period from 1922 to 1925 gave much attention to policy that did not involve the Far East.[31] Relations with Japan remained crisis-oriented and Hughes believed the crisis over. But other issues in the 1920s brought trouble to Hughes's tune of cooperation and by 1931 presented a very different situation. One of these was the problem of immigration, which in 1924 came to a screeching halt as a topic of diplomatic negotiation with passage of the Japanese exclusion act. Despite increased Japanese–American trade, and partially because of fear of Japanese economic might, there was great pressure to prevent any further Japanese immigration. Hughes opposed such legislation, but perhaps contributed to its passage by encouraging the Japanese to express concern. A Japanese note, which forecast possible "grave consequences" was used by exclusionists in their campaign. Hughes wrote Senator Henry Cabot Lodge shortly after Congress acted:

> It is a dangerous thing to plant a deep feeling of resentment in the Japanese people, not that we need to apprehend, much less fear, war, but that we shall have hereafter in the East to count upon a sense of injury and antagonism instead of friendship and cooperation. I dislike to think what the reaping will be after the sowing of this seed.[32]

The reaction in Japan was very strong. Some combined it with the Washington Conference. After the 1924 crisis, more and more "the Washington Conference structure of international relations which the civilian government upheld was seen as a white-sponsored system for the perpetuation of Western domination of the world."[33] Many now called for an independent Japanese policy. Another troublesome issue was China, which was so unsettled in the 1920s that cooperation on Chinese questions by the United States and Japan, along with Britain, proved difficult, if not impossible.

The years after Hughes left the State Department saw a movement away from cooperation with the Japanese, especially in China. Hughes's successor, Frank B. Kellogg, turned to more unilateral action in regard to China. American sympathies toward China intensified again, especially after 1928.[34] China increasingly was becoming a separate issue in Japanese–American relations. Still, it was not until the Manchurian crisis of 1931 that the residue of good feeling from the Washington attempt at new Japanese–American relations was washed away.

The period from 1931 to 1941 has recently been subjected to a good deal of analysis, with a resulting deeper understanding. Among the most important American personalities dominating Japanese–American relations of this era was Henry L. Stimson, secretary of state from 1929 to 1933 and then secretary of war from 1940 to 1945. In contrast to Hughes, Stimson had had some experience in foreign affairs when he entered the State Department. A lawyer by training and a young member of the circle around Theodore Roosevelt, he had served as secretary of war under President Taft, went to Nicaragua in 1927 for President Coolidge and then became governor general of the Philippines in 1928.[35] His legal training was evident in his approach to foreign affairs. In his career in local and national government he had perceived the power of public opinion, and believed that it could be an instrument of diplomacy "to support righteousness in world politics. The decent and aroused feelings of mankind would stand behind an honest diplomacy and perhaps work wonders in world affairs."[36] He was representative of the feeling in the United States after the World War that it was possible to use world democratic opinion in support of diplomacy. He believed that nations had to fulfill obligations. Should they stray, there was always public opinion. In sum, "Stimson's ideal world was one of ordered and disciplined relations between states according to standards set by a stern Christianity and an Anglo–Saxon sense of proper procedures."[37]

Stimson came into office with some definite ideas about the Far East, the result of his experience there. He believed the United States had a major interest in East Asia. The position of the United States, he felt, was greatly strengthened by the existence of an outpost in the Philippines, where he thought continued American leadership necessary. Stimson believed "complete independence from the United States was the wrong final goal for the Philippines; he considered it impractical and unrealistic; he believed it neither useful for the Filipinos nor advantageous to the United States." His goal for the Philippines was "self-government under American protection." These views meant major involvement in Asia. He did recognize Japanese rights in the Far East but put limits on them. He opposed any extension of Japanese rights in China, especially in Manchuria. When the Manchurian crisis broke out in 1931, he saw it as an issue "between the Chinese aspiration toward complete national independence and the Japanese conviction that security of basic Japanese interests required the maintenance of extensive economic and political rights in Manchuria."[38] From the day he entered office he favored the former. One other point must be made. Stimson came away from the Philippines with certain views about the Oriental mind. His experience had led him to the conclusion that Orientals "had to be faced with firmness, a show of force and a demonstrable willingness to use it."[39]

It was in 1931 that the relationship between the United States and Japan changed. And in that year Stimson began to play his tune, "Stop the Aggression," which he sounded for the rest of the decade. At the same time, the Japanese began to play their own music as they sought to overcome the effects of the Great Depression and chart their own course in East Asia. The Manchurian crisis that began in September of that year was the beginning of the end of the peaceful relations between the United States and Japan. It brought American attention back to the Far East and renewed sympathy for China. It also symbolized a course of aggression by Japan in East Asia that was a threat to American interests there.

The reasons for the change in Japanese policy in 1931 have been well documented.[40] The economic crisis resulting from the depression; decision by Japanese militarists and nationalists to pursue a new course; resentment against the Western-dominated policy of "International Cooperation"; lack of benefits from existing economic relations with China, especially given Chinese efforts to break Japanese dominance in Manchuria; together with Pan–Asian beliefs and many other forces all came together in a war of conquest in Manchuria. From the first Stimson expressed alarm, but considered caution necessary to aid the civil Japanese leaders who were struggling against the militarists who precipitated the crisis. By January 1932, more than three months after the Japanese began their movement in Manchuria, Stimson was ready to act. He saw the crisis as larger than just Manchuria and believed "that the peace of the Orient was his business, for if a Far Eastern nation broke the peace on a large scale the precedent would not be lost upon Europe, and out of a widening series of international crises would come eventually a crisis in world order."[41] Most of his fellow diplomats saw him as an alarmist.

Stimson had hoped that the matter could be solved by the League of Nations, and even sent a representative to a league council meeting with instructions to participate in any discussion of the Kellogg–Briand Treaty. He had been hopeful when the Japanese consented to a league investigating commission, but wondered if in Japan "the cause of Mr. Hyde against Dr. Jekyll has in large measure been victorious." His fears were confirmed on January 2, 1932, when the Japanese took Chinchow, and he decided the United States had to act unilaterally. On January 7 he asked for nonrecognition, the same policy used by the United States at the time of the Twenty-One Demands: The United States

> cannot admit the legality of any situation *de facto* nor does it intend to recognize any treaty or agreement entered into between those Governments, or agents thereof, which may impair the treaty rights of the United States or its citizens in China, including those which relate to the sovereignty, the independence, or the territorial and administrative integrity of the Republic of China, nor to the international policy relative to China, commonly known as the open door policy; and that it does not intend to recognize any situation, treaty, or agreement which may be brought about by means contrary to the covenants and obligations of the Pact of Paris of August 27, 1928, to which Treaty both China and Japan, as well as the United States, are parties.[42]

Stimson's policy had President Hoover's agreement, with both aware of the danger should Japan persist. The Stimson Doctrine, as nonrecognition became known, became part of Japanese–American relations. Reaction was not positive. Britain and France, not consulted before the doctrine was announced, had other concerns. The Japanese response seemed a full-fledged assault on Shanghai. After diplomatic efforts, Stimson determined to state the American position with regard to the Japanese attack upon Shanghai (which had begun at the end of January) and used the device of a public letter to Senator William E. Borah. The letter of February 23, 1932 went beyond the doctrine of January 7 by indicating that the United States saw the Japanese move as a violation of the Nine-Power Treaty which might result in the abrogation of the whole Washington system.[43] Stimson was perhaps prepared to go further, with the possible introduction of economic sanctions, but President Hoover and the American people were not. They were interested in too many other things. While Stimson's beliefs were strengthened when the assembly of the league, after receiving the report of the Lytton Commission, condemned Japan, the Japanese response was to withdraw from the league.

In the end Stimson's policy failed. Without the resort to economic sanctions or force there was little that could have been expected. Most Americans condemned Japan but saw little in the interest of the United States which would justify more than condemnation. The Japanese ignored Stimson's opposition, except as a way of gaining domestic support. But Stimson was to have more influence than he might have expected, for his stand attracted some very influential Americans. Most important, he found a receptive audience with Hoover's successor in the White House, Franklin D. Roosevelt. With family ties to China and a strong interest in the navy, Roosevelt shared Stimson's concern about Japan. In several conversations he assured Stimson of continuity on the nonrecognition theme. The President-to-be refused at this time to go the sanction route with Stimson, but he also refused to legitimitize Japan's change of the status quo in Asia. FDR adopted Stimson's tune of "Stop the Aggression."[44] While other considerations were to become more important in the 1930s—naval rivalry, worldwide aggression, Japan's move southward—Stimson set FDR on the route to a collision with Japan. Throughout the 1930s, China complicated Japanese–American relations. The United States wanted the Japanese to return to the 1920s role in China. Chinese problems "dominated attempts to find a way to avoid war. Traditional China policy had a paralyzing effect on diplomacy."[45]

It was appropriate that Stimson returned to the cabinet in July 1940, for by then his policy had gained much acceptance, both within the administration and among the people. Stimson out of office had continued to urge sanctions. In October 1937, in the wake of Japanese aggression upon China, he appealed for a governmental ban on trade with Japan. But FDR still hoped for peace. By 1940 things were different, and Stimson added his voice to those advocating a hard line against Japanese moves in the Pacific. His view of the

Oriental mind reappeared. He told the British ambassador in August of that year that "to get on with Japan one had to treat her rough, unlike other countries." He told President Roosevelt the same thing, that history had "shown that when the United States indicates by clear language and bold actions that she intends to carry out a clear and affirmative policy in the Far East, Japan will yield to that policy even though it conflicts with her own Asiatic policy and conceived interest."[46] When the Japanese seemed to become part of a broader threat to America in the Far East and Europe, the American people and Roosevelt shared his views. The Japanese response came on December 7, 1941.

Was the war inevitable? That is a difficult question, about which much has been written. A conference of American and Japanese historians, at Hakone, Japan, July 14–18, 1969, dealt with that question by looking at both the Japanese and American governments. Publication of the proceedings of that conference will be an interesting account of this question.[47] There were individuals within both governments seeking compromise, and opportunities for peaceful resolution of difficulties that each government missed on the route to Pearl Harbor. The most striking fact to me is the expectation that began to develop in the leaders and people of each country that war was inevitable. The United States always had hesitated in its disagreements with the Japanese—war was not worth the interests in dispute. By the late 1930s this feeling had begun to disappear. The 1930s began with a Great Depression but no widespread feeling that war would come. By 1941 feeling had changed.

These four spokesmen represent the changing American views of Japan and the changing roles of the United States and Japan as perceived in Washington. To be sure, Japanese–American relations were not given constant attention. But out of the crisis diplomacy, a change had occurred. In the movement from a view that was a mix of fear and respect, to the view that Japan was an aggressor nation dominated by the military, the relationship had gone sour. In the years between 1898 and 1941, the Japanese had danced to the tunes of TR, Wilson and Hughes, but they would not dance to that played by Stimson. It was ironic that one of the erstwhile members of Theodore Roosevelt's circle should have become the instrumentalist of the new tune. One wonders if the Republican Roosevelt would have liked it.

NOTES TO CHAPTER SEVEN

1. There are a number of surveys of Japanese-American relations. Most valuable for this study were Ernest R. May and James C. Thomson, Jr., eds., *American–East Asian Relations: A Survey* (Cambridge: Harvard University Press, 1972), which includes essays by Raymond Esthus, Charles Neu, Burton Beers, Roger Dingman, Akira Iriye, Waldo Heinrichs and Louis Morton, covering the period from 1901 to 1941; William Neumann, *America Encounters Japan: From Perry to*

MacArthur (Baltimore: The Johns Hopkins Press, 1963); Akira Iriye, *Across the Pacific: An Inner History of American–East Asian Relations* (New York: Harcourt, Brace & World, Inc., 1967); Edwin Reischauer, *The United States and Japan* (Cambridge: Harvard University Press, 1965); and three olders accounts, Foster Rhea Dulles, *Forty Years of American–Japanese Relations* (New York: D. Appleton–Century Co., 1937); A Whitney Griswold, *The Far Eastern Policy of the United States* (New York: Harcourt, Brace, 1938); and Tyler Dennett, *Americans in Eastern Asia* (New York: Macmillan, 1922).

2. There is now a good deal of discussion about different phases in Japanese–American relations before 1941. Professor Iriye in his *Across the Pacific,* and in two other books—*After Imperialism: The Search for a New Order in the Far East, 1921–1931* (Cambridge: Harvard University Press, 1965) and *Pacific Estrangement: Japanese and American Expansion, 1897–1911* (Cambridge: Harvard University Press, 1972)—has done the best job of distinguishing the different phases, and his works are essential for anyone interested in that subject.

3. Waldo Heinrichs, "1931–1937," in May and Thomson, eds., *American–East Asian Relations,* pp. 258–259.

4. This class held a reunion in 1922 in Tokyo, with the American members going on board the U.S.S. *Henderson,* along with the Secretary of the Navy, Edwin Denby, who though not a member of the class had lived in Asia. For an account of the reuinion, see Eugene P. Trani, "Secretary Denby Takes a Trip," *Michigan History* LI (1967): 277–297.

5. Akira Iriye's new book, *Pacific Estrangement,* is an excellent account of the expansionist collision after 1897.

6. There are a number of works dealing with Roosevelt and his view of Japan. Among the best are two works by Raymond Esthus, *Theodore Roosevelt and the International Rivalries* (Waltham, Massachusetts: Ginn–Blaisdell, 1970) and *Theodore Roosevelt and Japan* (Seattle: University of Washington Press, 1966); and books by Charles Neu, *An Uncertain Friendship: Theodore and Japan, 1906–1909* (Cambridge: Harvard University Press, 1967) and Howard K. Beale, *Theodore Roosevelt and the Rise of America to World Power* (Baltimore: The Johns Hopkins Press, 1956). Shorter attempts to analyze Roosevelt's view on foreign policy, giving some attention to his East Asian policy, are David Healy's excellent "Theodore Roosevelt and the Sturdy Virtues," in his book *U.S. Expansionism* (Madison: University of Wisconsin Press, 1970) and Eugene P. Trani, "Theodore Roosevelt," in Frank Merli and Theodore Wilson, eds., *Makers of American Diplomacy 1775–1975,* (forthcoming, 1974, New York: Charles Scribner's Sons).

7. For an account of the role TR played in ending this war, see Eugene P. Trani, *The Treaty of Portsmouth: An Adventure in American Diplomacy* (Lexington: University of Kentucky Press, 1969).

8. As cited in William Neumann, *America Encounters Japan,* p. 118. Raymond Esthus's *Theodore Roosevelt and the International Rivalries* has a good discussion of TR's effort to defuse the issues separating the United States and Japan.

9. TR to Philander C. Knox, February 8, 1909, in Elting E. Morison, ed., *The Letters of Theodore Roosevelt,* 8 vols. (Cambridge: Harvard University Press, 1951–1954), VI: 1510–1514.

10. For a fine discussion of the Japanese decision to move to continental expansion, see Akira Iriye, *Pacific Estrangement.*

11. Ibid., especially pp. 169–201.

12. Charles Neu, "1906–1913," in May and Thomson, eds., *American–East Asian Relations,* p. 159.

13. Woodrow Wilson, *History of the American People,* 5 vols. (New York: Harper & Brothers, 1902), V: 296, and a news report from the Waterbury, *American,* December 13, 1900, in Arthur Link et al., eds., *The Papers of Woodrow Wilson,* vol. XII (Princeton: Princeton University Press, 1972), pp. 46–48.

14. William Neumann, *America Encounters Japan,* pp. 140–141.

15. Woodrow Wilson to Daniel Coit Gilman, April 13, 1889, in Arthur Link et al., eds., *The Papers of Woodrow Wilson,* vol. VI (1969), pp. 169–172.

16. For the Wilson comments about Chinese immigration, see Wilson, *History of the American People,* V: 185. There are a number of accounts of Wilson's Far Eastern policy. Among the most valuable are Roy Watson Curry, *Woodrow Wilson and Far Eastern Policy* (New York: Bookman Associates, 1957); Tien-yi Li, *Woodrow Wilson's China Policy, 1913–1917* (New York: Twayne Publishers, Inc., 1952); and Russell H. Fifield, *Woodrow Wilson and the Far East: The Diplomacy of the Shantung Question* (New York: Thomas Y. Crowell Company, 1952). The best treatment of Wilson's attitudes toward diplomacy is Arthur S. Link, *Wilson the Diplomatist: A Look at His Major Foreign Policies* (Baltimore: The Johns Hopkins Press, 1957), which should, of course, be supplemented with Professor Link's definitive biography of Wilson, now completed to 1917.

17. Woodrow Wilson to Edward C. Jenkins, March 17, 1913, Woodrow Wilson MSS, Library of Congress. For an analysis of the influence of missionaries on Wilson's China policy, see Eugene P. Trani, "Woodrow Wilson, China, and the Missionaries, 1913–1921," *Journal of Presbyterian History* XLIX (1971): 328–351.

18. William Neumann, *America Encounters Japan,* p. 136.

19. Burton Beers, "1913–1917," in May and Thomson, eds., *American–East Asian Relations,* p. 183. Beers has written a fine study, *Vain Endeavor: Robert Lansing's Attempts to End the American–Japanese Rivalry* (Durham: Duke University Press, 1962).

20. Roger Dingman, "1917–1922," in May and Thomson, eds., *American–East Asian Relations,* p. 199.

21. See Russell Fifield, *Woodrow Wilson and the Far East,* for a treatment of the Shantung issue at the Paris Conference.
22. Wilson to S. I. Woodbridge, September 2, 1919, J. S. Woodbridge Collection, copy in Princeton University Library.
23. John V. A. MacMurray to Roland Morris, February 7, 1920, Roland Morris MSS, Library of Congress.
24. Betty Glad, *Charles Evans Hughes and the Illusions of Innocence: A Study in American Diplomacy* (Urbana: University of Illinois Press, 1966), pp. 153–162 and pp. 281–303. Two other studies of Hughes are Merlo Pusey, *Charles Evans Hughes* 2 vols. (New York: Macmillan, 1951); and Dexter Perkins, *Charles Evans Hughes and American Democratic Statesmanship* (Boston: Little, Brown, 1956).
25. Akira Iriye, *After Imperialism,* pp. 1–30, Professor Iriye develops this model of "International Cooperation" very ably in *After Imperialism* and is especially helpful on Japanese reaction.
26. Betty Glad, *Charles Evans Hughes and the Illusions of Innocence,* p. 287 and p. 292.
27. Ibid., p. 297.
28. Harold and Margaret Sprout, *Towards a New Order of Seapower* (Princeton: Princeton University Press, 1943).
29. L. Ethan Ellis, *Republican Foreign Policy: 1921–1933* (New Brunswick, N. J.: Rutgers University Press, 1968), p. 107. Another recent treatment of the Washington Conference is Thomas H. Buckley, *The United States and the Washington Conference, 1921–1922* (Knoxville: University of Tennessee Press, 1970).
30. Akira Iriye, *After Imperialism,* p. 36. This study is excellent on the different reactions in Japan to the Washington system.
31. Hughes spent, for example, much time on Latin America after 1922. A brief survey of his efforts there is Eugene P. Trani, "Charles Evans Hughes: The First Good Neighbor," *Northwest Ohio Quarterly* XL (1968): 138–152.
32. As cited in Akira Iriye, *After Imperialism,* p. 35. See also William Neumann, *America Encounters Japan,* pp. 176–177.
33. Akira Iriye, *Across the Pacific,* p. 153.
34. For a treatment of Kellogg's policy, see Dorothy Borg, *American Policy and the Chinese Revolution, 1925–1928* (New York: Octagon Books, 1968).
35. There are a number of treatments of Stimson. Among the most helpful is Robert H. Ferrell, *Frank B. Kellogg–Henry L. Stimson* (New York: Cooper Square Publishers, Inc., 1963).
36. Ibid., p. 164.
37. William Neumann, *America Encounters Japan,* p. 191.
38. McGeorge Bundy, *On Active Service in Peace and War* (New York: Harper & Brothers, 1948), pp. 146–150 and p. 221.
39. William Neumann, *America Encounters Japan,* p. 191.
40. See Akira Iriye, "1922–1931," and Waldo Heinrichs, "1931–1937," in May and Thomson, eds., *American–East Asian Relations,* for bibliography on this subject.

41. Robert H. Ferrell, *Frank B. Kellogg–Henry L. Stimson*, p. 219. The best single account of the Manchurian Crisis is Robert H. Ferrell, *American Diplomacy in the Great Depression: Hoover–Stimson Foreign Policy, 1929–1933* (New Haven: Yale University Press, 1957). See also Armin Rappaport, *Henry L. Stimson and Japan, 1931–1933* (Chicago: University of Chicago Press, 1963) and Richard Current, *Secretary Stimson: A Study in Statecraft* (New Brunswick, N. J.: Rutgers University Press, 1954).

42. As cited in Robert Ferrell, *Frank B. Kellogg–Henry L. Stimson,* p. 235, and pp. 238–239.

43. Ibid, pp. 253–255.

44. For an account of FDR's relations with Stimson, see William Neumann, *America Encounters Japan,* pp. 199–201 and pp. 263–265. A detailed analysis of the impact that the Manchurian Crisis had on Franklin D. Roosevelt, as well as the influence that Stimson had with the President-elect, appears in William Neumann, "Franklin D. Roosevelt and Japan, 1913–1933," *Pacific Historical Review* XXII (May 1953): 143–153. Neumann shows that this crisis made FDR very suspicious of Japan, and again made China a major consideration of Japanese–American relations for Roosevelt.

45. Waldo Heinrichs, "The Griswold Theory of Our Far Eastern Policy: A Commentary," in Dorothy Borg, comp., *Historians and American Far Eastern Policy* (New York: Columbia University East Asian Institute, 1966), p. 41.

46. As cited in William Neumann, *American Encounters Japan,* pp. 263–265.

47. This volume was published in 1973, by the Columbia University Press, under the title: *Pearl Harbor as History: Japanese–American Relations, 1931–1941,* edited by Dorothy Borg and Shumpei Okamoto. An excellent survey of the last complicated few years before the war is Louis Morton, "1937–1941," in May and Thomson, eds., *American–East Asian Relations.*

Chapter Eight

Expectations and Developing Attitudes in the Pacific

Akira Iriye

To understand the nature of what is new in the current emerging order in Asia, it seems almost axiomatic that we have to go back to history to gain some historical perspective. My view is that by understanding the nature of the conflict between the United States and Japan which culminated in the Pacific War, we can understand a great deal about the postwar world, especially the postwar relations between the two countries. Also, we can try to gain some sense of what it is that is new in present-day Japanese–American relations. Without that kind of perspective, we would simply be speculating as to what is new in general, rather than what may be of the more persistent, more enduring aspects of postwar relations between our countries.

To understand the nature of the Pacific War and the nature of the American–Japanese conflict, I suggest that we deal with the war not simply as a unidimentional phenomenon, but that we at least look at four factors, four ingredients, or four aspects of the Japanese–American conflict.

The first of these is perhaps the most commonly seen aspect: the clash between Japanese and American national interests. It is common—I think it is almost totally logical—to say that the war arose between the two countries because Japanese and American national interests in the Pacific collided. Having said that, one really has not said very much, because then we have to ask the question: what worldly national interests of the two countries were such that they had to eventuate in war? Here, I think historians have done a great deal of research about the nature of the Japanese–American crisis in terms of national interests. I think it is fair to say that there really was no fundamental conflict, in terms of national interests narrowly defined—that is, in terms of security or in terms of immediate interests—because Japan was not threatening the United States by any kind of naval action. Up until 1941, there was no awareness on the American side that Japan was in a position to immediately menace American security. Neither was the United States threatening Japanese security at this time.

The same pattern persisted regarding mutual economic interests in China. There was really no fundamental collision of national interests of Japan and the United States in China, because throughout the twentieth century the United States was neither in a position to nor willing to oppose Japanese policy in China.

To the extent that there is a national interest factor here, I think one has to talk about Japan's economic interests as the Japanese perceived these economic interests, that is, from the point of view of the Japanese in the late 1930s up through 1941. Japan is so totally dependent upon the supply of raw materials from abroad, that from the Japanese point of view, this was an essential national interest.

The idea in 1941 was, of course, that Japan had to obtain raw materials somewhere. Some came from Manchuria in China, but it was found that that was not enough, especially in terms of oil, rubber, tin and so on. Some could have been and had been obtained in the United States. But if, because of the gradual tightening of American policy, this was impossible, then, from the Japanese point of view, Japan had to turn elsewhere, to Southeast Asia or the southwestern Pacific. If we are talking about the clash of national interests between two countries, there was a genuine clash in this sense. The Japanese had a self-perceived need for raw materials, and the United States denied Japanese southern expansion and, therefore, denied Japan much-needed raw materials. This was one factor which was to lead to direct hostility.

One fundamental aspect of the Japanese–American crisis was the fact that the Pacific relationship between the two countries became merged with the European crisis after 1939 and certainly after 1940. Therefore, American–Japanese relations became part of the global conflict between the Axis powers. Therefore, the issue as of 1941 was not simply one in which Japan wanted to obtain raw materials in Southeast Asia in ways of which the United States did not approve. More fundamentally, there was the question as to the future of Asia and the Pacific, and the future of the Asian Pacific international order. Was Japan going to be the predominant power on the continent of Asia?

Therefore, the primary concern here was what was going to be the future of the Southeast Asia–Southwestern Pacific region. The Japanese decision after 1940 was to take advantage of the European war. It was going to ally itself to the Axis powers in Europe and to establish hegemony in this region. The global political vision that Japan had of itself—as a superpower of tremendous strength and hegemony over the whole of the Southeast Asia–Southwestern Pacific region—obviously came into conflict with the American globalism—American power politics. But this conflict was not really related to the immediate needs of national interests.

There is the view that the United States was, and must remain, as Asian Pacific power. In order to do that, the United States must stand in the way of Japan's attempt to establish hegemony in that region. World domination was seen as part of the global conspiracy on the part of the Axis powers. Therefore, from the American point of view, Japanese action was viewed as part of the struggle for a new order between the Axis powers on one hand and the Anglo–American powers on the other. The United States was trying to maintain a global status quo, a global equilibrium against the attack on it by the Axis powers in Europe. Therefore, it followed that the same attempt by Japan had to be resisted. This is a much more globalistic than nationalistic notion.

Thus the United States felt it should be concerned with Asian Pacific affairs even if these affairs have no immediate relevance to America's needs. It was necessary for America to assert its position and power in this region, because this was part of the American global strategy. These two aspects of American–Japanese relations—existing national interests and emerging global interests—formed a very important part of the beginning of the crisis between the two countries.

I would go a step beyond this and argue that there were two other important factors in the Japanese–American crisis. One is the ideological aspect. In addition to global power politics and national interests and their collision in the Pacific, there is the fact that the crisis between the two countries symbolized a conflict between two ideologies. Japan supported an ideology of Pan–Asianism in the 1930s. As an Asian country, standing for Asian liberation from Western colonialism, Japan was trying to establish a new Asian order of Asian peoples and was going to expel Western influence, Western peoples and Western ideas from Asia. This was going to be a new world.

From the American point of view, of course, this was to be resisted. Asia was not to fall under Japanese hegemony. Asia was an area in which the United States wished still to espouse universal principles—such as self-determination, imperialism and freedom—that had been written into the Atlantic Charter in August 1941. These were not viewed as simply Atlantic principles to be applied only to Western countries; they also applied to the Pacific nations. Therefore, there was a fundamental collision, a fundamental crisis, between Japan's Pan–Asian doctrine and America's more universalistic doctrine.

There really could be no accommodation, because this involved, among other things, the question of China. From the Japanese point of view, China was an Asian country that ought to be governed by Asian precepts, and Japan was going to provide these principles. China was going to behave the way that the Japanese told it to behave. From the American point of view, China was not simply another Asian country. It was a country to which the principles of the Atlantic Charter ought to apply. Thus, on the one hand, there was the United States, still trying to work within the framework of traditional Western diplomacy—the League of Nations, the Wilsonian principles; while on the other hand there was Japan, which had rejected Western precepts and was trying to establish a new order of Pan—Asianism.

This leads to the fourth and final aspect of Japanese–American crisis. Ultimately, there was an extra dimension, for in addition to ideology, power politics and national interests, there is also that rather vaguely defined, amorphous area of two nations' mutual ignorance, misunderstandings and misperceptions. Fundamentally there was a crisis because the two peoples represented two different cultural traditions and two different historical backgrounds. There is a great deal of chauvinism and general phobia on both sides resulting from each nation's ignorance of the other.

When one looks at the 1930s, I think that many of the outstanding features are clear. There is the fact that mutual knowledge of one another or association with one another was extremely limited. The great realm of mutual hostility, chauvinism and general phobia was not related to immediate circumstances in the 1930s, although that was important too, but more to the way the two peoples had developed as separate peoples—in terms of their ways of life and in terms of their cultures.

The result was that there was, in particular, a sense of injury built into Japanese perceptions of the United States both due to the immigration crisis that went back to the Russian–Japanese War, and more particularly, to the un-Oriental, un-Japanese Immigration Act of 1924.

It is quite remarkable that on the American side nobody thought very much of it. When the Immigration Act of 1924 was passed there was a moment of hesitation, but people soon forgot about it. A thing like that has a tremendous impact, as one realizes when one reads Japanese writings and speeches about American–Japanese relations in the twenties and thirties. One is impressed by the constant references to America's immigration policy and by the sense of self-injury—that the United States was not quite treating Japan as an equal nation. There is also a kind of racial consciousness which viewed the United States as unfair, arrogant and materialistic. This last was a product of the experience of the depression.

On the American side, there is an unfavorable image of Japan and the Japanese, again going back to the turn of the century. There is the sense that Japan, despite its superficial Westernization, was an extremely feudal, extremely uncivilized society. This kind of psychological-emotional factor, while not articulated, was, nevertheless, always there in the 1930s.

When one talks about the Pacific war, one has to talk in terms of these four dimensions: the collision of national interests; the Japanese and American searches for a new Pacific order; the ideological confrontation; and the psychological dimension of this. This kind of background—this kind of approach—might enable us to see more clearly what has happened since the end of the war in 1945.

First of all, the Pacific war put an end to the Japanese dream of a new Asian empire. The Pacific war brought about the tremendous growth of American power and the emergence of the United States as the predominant Asian–Pacific power. Since the Yalta conference of 1945, a new balance emerged in Asia primarily between the United States and the Soviet Union. In the new definition of the Asian international system, Japan was, of course, relegated to a minor status; the United States took control over the Japanese islands and also established its hegemony over Japan proper. Until 1952, Japan was occupied by the United States. Even after the peace treaty, Japan was integrated into the American system of Asian balance. There was a tremendous reversal, a tremendous transformation, in the global power–political aspect of American–Japanese relations.

Since about 1970, America's predominant position in the Western Pacific and East Asia has been somewhat changed. This transformation has to do more with China than with Japan. The Nixon–Kissinger policy of upholding China and recognizing China as a great Asian power has resulted in Japan's self-conscious assertion that it, too, is a great Asian power. This is a new development in Japanese consciousness. For a long time after 1945, the earlier self-image that Japan was going to be the predominant Asian power had been totally shattered, replaced by the postwar image of the United States as Japan's protector and of Japan as being part of the American definition of the Asian order.

This has changed somewhat since 1970 not because the Japanese began to think of themselves once again as a great power, but only because the United States recognized China as a great power. Since the United States was going to recognize China as a great Asian power, the Japanese felt they, too, would like to have this status. This is very strange, because they did not initiate this self-consciousness. It all came indirectly because of the Kissinger–Nixon trips to China. Therefore, it is not surprising that the Japanese, on the whole, even today do not seem to have a very clear idea of what it is that they mean by Japan's great power status.

It does seem to be likely that in terms of real military power Japan will still be overshadowed by the United States, the Soviet Union and perhaps by China. If we take this historical perspective, there will not be a return to the situation before 1941 of Japan and the United States once again trying to struggle for supremacy in the Western Pacific. For some time to come, anyway, Japan will be content to be part of the American security system. Therefore, we can take care of this aspect of Japanese–American relations when we say that a new order is emerging in the Asian Pacific region. I do not really see much new in terms of global politics, because the Japanese have other choices—the 1935 choice and the postwar pattern. It seems clear that, despite this new consciousness of Japan as a power in terms of the total picture of Asian–Pacific system, Japan will still remain part of the overall American system.

The second aspect which I mentioned was the national interest aspect. Apart from the more general pattern of global diplomacy, there are more pragmatic, narrowly defined national interests of the United States and of Japan. We have seen collision. We have seen competition. We have had all kinds of practical issues in which the two countries have been at odds. The initiative has come, on the whole, from the Japanese side. Since 1945, the Japanese have developed a very clearly articulated sense of what their country needs. Paradoxically, there is no basic difference between what has been perceived since 1945 and what used to be perceived in the 1930s.

In terms of immediate national interests, what the Japanese have always needed were raw materials and overseas markets. There is no difference between what they wanted in the thirties and what they want today. The only difference is in means; the ends remain the same. Since 1945, the Japanese have turned to peaceful methods of economic development and expansion. The same drive still exists, and this has brought about some growing tension and friction between the United States and Japan. Immediately after the war, for about fifteen or twenty years, there was no basic conflict between Japan's economic diplomacy (referred to as economism of Japanese foreign policy), which has been the basic definition of Japanese national interests, and American policy. The United States also thought that it was in America's interests to encourage Japan's economic recovery and economic development. To have an economically stable, economically viable Japan fitted in with America's overall strategy in Asia.

More recently, in the past ten years or so, we have seen a growing concern in the United States that Japan's economistic foreign policy might compete with America's national interests, as Americans, too, are becoming more and more aware of the need for raw materials, overseas markets and investment opportunities. From the American point of view, Japan seems to be getting all the benefits of an American alliance while at the same time seeking to expand its economic opportunities and interests at the expense of the United States. Here again, we will have to argue that there is little new in Japan's basic economic drive, which has always existed. The need today, therefore, is not to ignore those areas of potential and actual competition between the two countries, but to find some areas where their respective national interests can still be made compatible. Given the national interests as narrowly defined, and these national interests are not likely to change immediately, it is really a task of statesmanship to see to it that they do not clash as they did toward the end of the 1930s but that they be made more compatible.

Fortunately, things may be different today because of the combination of all four factors that I have pointed out. In the 1930s, as I have shown, it was not simply national interests that brought about the war. War resulted because the conflict in national interests was combined with other factors. That is why it is necessary to go beyond national interest considerations and power-politics considerations and look at some other factors as well.

This leads to the third factor, the third ingredient, in Japanese–American relations—the ideological aspect. Here one can say that there has truly been a change in Japanese–American relations. In contrast to the fundamental collision between Japan's Pan–Asianist orientation and America's Atlantic Charter orientation which brought about the war in 1941 and which characterized their relations in the 1940s, there has been some change, especially on the Japanese side. Perhaps there has not been that much change on the American side, because on the American side there still seems to be Atlantic Charter type of consciousness. It is a good thing to speak for self-determination, independence, democracy and freedom. I do not really see that much has changed in American thinking about those principles.

On the Japanese side, there has been a radical reversal of Japanese thinking to the extent that pacifism or antimilitarism replaced in 1945 the doctrine of military expansionism. What has replaced militarism is not anti-expansionism; the Japanese are still expansionistic. What they have now is an ideology of economic expansionism or peaceful expansionism rather than militaristic expansionism. But within this new ideology of peaceful or economic expansion and pacifistic foreign policy, the Japanese will still be committed to expansion unless something very drastic happens.

Instead of the rabid anti-Western phobia and chauvinistic Pan–Asianism, the Japanese after 1945 once again returned to Western civilization. I say returned rather than adopted, because for some time since the mid-nineteenth century they had identified themselves with Western civilization. They reacted against that in the 1930s. Since 1945, they have come back to Western civilization. They have adopted the Anglo–American principles of the Atlantic Charter written into the MacArthur-given new constitution, which the Japanese still regard as their own. There is the sense that Japan now has been restored as a member of a civilized community of nations. This has meant, in Japanese eyes, primarily a Western-defined community of nations.

Of course, it is not really as simple as that, because there is a residue of Asianist sentiment. Japan, after all, is still in Asia. There are things which are not quite reducible to simply creations of Western international relations. There is, I think, a great sense of guilt vis à vis China and the rest of Asia. I have often wondered why it is that the Japanese feel more guilty toward the Chinese than toward the Americans. Despite the fact that Japan fought against both the United States and China, they really feel somewhat more guilty toward the Chinese than toward Westerners. The sense of guilt and shame—toward other Asians and especially toward the Chinese—is extremely intense. That may have to do with some sense of Asianism. More recently, Tanaka's trip to China indicated that there is some sentiment of Asian friendliness and neighborliness.

When I say that Japan has returned to Western civilization, it does not mean that there is no ambiguity there. There is an ambivalence in Japanese sentiment, but there is no rabid doctrine of Pan–Asianism such as we saw in the

1930s. Therefore, I do see some hope that some American ideas and some Japanese ideas are comptaible today to the extent that they were not compatible in the 1930s and '40s. Most of the ideas can coexist. Therefore, we ought to encourage this trend, which is new in the sense that this is a post–1945 phenomenon. It does seem very important for the two countries to continue to struggle, to search for a definition of Japanese–American relations in which their respective ideologies can cooperate and promote mutual peace and prosperity.

Finally, there is the psychological-emotional aspect of Japanese–American relations. Ultimately, one has to recognize the mass of people, both in Japan and the United States, to whom the other three factors may mean nothing. Ninety-five percent of Americans and ninety-five percent of Japanese may have no awareness of national interests, ideologies or global politics, yet they have to deal with one another. It is here that one has to deal in terms of a rather vague sense of mutual images, mutual attitudes towards one another, emotions, prejudices, ignorance, and that sort of thing. Here too, it seems that many things have happened. The Pacific war, of course, saw the height of mutual hostility and antagonism which was carried to some extremes because of wartime propaganda—movies, novels and so on, portraying each other as monsters.

That has changed since 1945. On the American side, there has been the gradual lessening of wartime hostility. For a time after 1945, Japan was viewed as a ward, as a protectee of the United States or as a country that was to be transformed in the image of the United States. Of course, MacArthur personified this sense that the United States was going to bring democracy and christianity to Japan. By 1947, MacArthur was saying that Japan had transformed itself. This optimism characterized one aspect of the American image of Japan after the war. Japan had committed a crime; now it was being regenerated by the American occupation.

More recently, the pendulum may have swung once again to the idea of conflict. Morton Halperin of the Brookings Institute has postulated that, on the American side, there is a swinging of the pendulum back and forth between the image of Japan and the United States as in a state of inevitable conflict to one of inevitable harmony. The image of inevitable conflict in the war was replaced after the war by an image of inevitable harmony. Now, in the 1970s, because of the common competition, there may be a swing back to inevitable conflict. It would be unfortunate if American images were to swing back and forth between these two extremes.

On the Japanese side, too, we still have to talk in terms of the transformation of wartime hostility to the postwar sense of dependence on the United States. This again has undergone some change because of the Nixon shocks, from a sense of extreme dependence on the United States to some sense of uneasiness because of perceived changes in the United States. This is a psychological-emotional dimension which cannot be ignored.

American–Japanese relations since 1941, having exhibited these different dimensions, cannot be dealt with by isolating one factor. We have to take into consideration all these factors. When we talk about the new image, the new order, in the Asian–Pacific region, we are talking about these different aspects. We are not simply talking about formal diplomacy and formal power politics. We are talking more about images and economic relations. If the two peoples, therefore, could somehow continue to cooperate to create an intellectual, an emotional atmosphere of mutual understanding, then I think they will have made a very important contribution to history in that two peoples of such diverse cultural backgrounds could still relate to one another in the common quest for a new international order.

Chapter Nine

Comments

Louis C. Morton

The excellent chapters by Professors Trani and Iriye approach the problem of U.S.–Japanese relations in entirely different ways. Essentially, Professor Trani has presented us with a time model of U.S.–Japanese relations in the period 1898–1941 consisting of four equal but differing compartments. He has taken the period with which he deals, approximately forty years, and divided it into four equal chronological units, each a decade in length. With each of these ten year units he has associated a slogan and an individual (i.e., Wilson and "Imperialism Is Over," 1909–1920); and attempted to recapitulate and to summarize its most important developments. This approach has several obvious advantages. The identification is a convenient device; it focuses on a single aspect of the period and enables one to get a clear picture of these four periods. But it also has some shortcomings, which will be discussed below.

Professor Iriye has approached the problem of U.S.–Japanese relations from an altogether different direction. In an earlier work, he made an important contribution to the study of the Far East by exploring the perceptions or roles of each of the major Pacific powers as a three-way relationship: the way the United States viewed China and Japan; the way China viewed the United States and Japan; and the way Japan viewed the United States and China. These complicated interrelationships or perception roles proved most illuminating in terms of the policy of each during this comparable period. Professor Iriye has used the same method in the present paper in an effort to analyze the complex forces which led to the Pacific War and which still affect the relationship of the United States and Japan. Implicit in his analysis is the comparison of the postwar period with the prewar situation and the potential for conflict between the two countries today. Like his earlier study, the present one is a notable contribution. It deals with national interests, international politics—power politics as he calls it, the ideological elements as they affect international relations, and the psychological-emotional factors that shape national attitudes and perception.

The approaches of both these scholars contribute substantially to a better understanding of the prewar relationship between the United States and Japan, and the forces that affect their relationship today. In Professor Iriye's view, China was central in the relationship between the United States and Japan during the prewar years, but he does not believe, as do many students of the period, that it was Japan's policies and actions in China that drew it increasingly into conflict and ultimately war with the United States. Rather, he argues that it was the Japanese move into Southeast Asia in 1940 and 1941 that led to the attack on Pearl Harbor and war between the two countries. Iriye's analysis, it seems to me, is a circular type of argument. Why did Japan go into Southeast Asia in the first place? What interests did the United States have in Southeast Asia that would impel it to go to war over Southeast Asia, but not over China? The answer to these questions lead inevitably to China and to Japan's search for the resources to support its operations there.

As far as Mr. Trani's model is concerned, there is a danger in breaking the forty year period into four separate and neat compartments and treating each as a distinct and discrete unit. This compartmentalization focuses on the differences and blurs the continuities. The whole question of periodicity in history is an intriguing one. Events do not fall into such neat patterns and it seems that to break down a forty year period so conveniently into four equal time spans does violence to the flow of history. It just does not seem realistic. One is impelled to seek other time frames, and there are several just as valid— perhaps more so. I understand that this division into decades is for convenience of analysis, but Professor Trani has failed to emphasize sufficiently the limitations of his model.

The fourth of his units, the decade from 1930 to 1940, seems to me perhaps somewhat more contrived than the others. Great emphasis is placed on Stimson, who serves to identify and give cohesion to the decade. True, Stimson was secretary of state at the beginning of the decade. But he had no office in the Roosevelt administration until 1940, when he was appointed secretary of war. How then did he shape foreign policy between 1932 and 1940? Though a private citizen after 1932, he undoubtedly talked with Roosevelt from time to time, but it was Roosevelt, not Stimson, who shaped foreign policy during these years. Further, Professor Trani's estimate of the influence of Stimson on Roosevelt with respect to foreign policy seems to be based on circumstance rather than strong evidence. The notion that Stimson propelled Roosevelt into opposition to Japan or into a course that led to war with Japan comes as a surprise. Stimson's views of Japan are well known; many scholars have covered that subject. But it is doubtful that President Roosevelt, whose forebears had close ties to China, needed to be pushed or guided into opposition to Japan's policy of expansion.

Professor Trani's approach tends to omit or blur important elements in this forty year relationship between Japan and the United States. For example, this model does not account for the Tydings–McDuffie Act and the movement for Philippine independence. If one considers Stimson in the role of the aggressor concerning the use of force in this 1930–40 decade, one must explain why the United States at the same time is getting out of the Far East, why it is giving up the Philippines, its main military base in the Far East. The entire role of the Philippines, which the United States acquired in 1898 and which occupied a central position in American army and navy strategy and war plans, is largely ignored in Mr. Trani's paper. He mentions it as an element in the first unit, 1898–1909, which was dominated by Theodore Roosevelt, and pretty much drops it thereafter. As the major American base in the Far East, the Philippines was of constant concern to our military planners and, in some respects, to such important State Department officials as Stanley Hornbeck.

There is an assumption in Mr. Trani's study that military planning reflects intentions. I hope that is not the case. If it were, the United States between 1903 and 1939 must have intended to fight every major power and many minor ones as well, for it had plans for a variety of such contingencies, including war with Britain, Germany, Canada, Mexico, China and Japan. Undoubtedly, American strategic planners have developed contingency plans for fighting wars in every important area of the world today and in every conceivable situation. If war does come, however, it will probably not be covered in any of the contingency plans.

It is interesting in this connection to note that when the United States went to war in 1941, the plan for war, RAINBOW 5, called for the primary effort in the Atlantic to defeat Germany first, before turning to the Pacific and Japan. But it was Japan that attacked the United States on December 7, not Germany. The United States did not go to war with Germany until December 11, but on December 7 the military chiefs put into effect RAIN-BOW 5, the war plan that called for the defeat of Germany first. One wonders what would have happened if Hitler had not declared war on the United States. Perhaps Roosevelt would have found himself with a plan for fighting a war with a nation with whom he was not at war, and would therefore have had to call for a declaration of war against Germany in order to carry out the war plan. Undoubtedly Hitler took him out of a difficult position.

I would like now, if I may, to return to Professor Iriye's study and his view of the effects of the Yalta Agreement on the balance of power in Asia. I have difficulty with his view of the matter, if I understand it correctly. It seems to me that initially Roosevelt, in his plans for the conduct of the war against Japan and in his hopes for the Far East in the postwar period, assigned a major role to China. That was the reason for General Stilwell's mission to China and for the program to train and supply thirty Chinese divisions that would be used to pin down the Japanese forces in China and Manchuria. Unlike Churchill, Roosevelt had high hopes for China's contribution in the war effort, accepted

U.S. responsibility for the China theater and supported Chiang throughout the war. The truth of the matter, which it took about two years and hundreds of messages from Stilwell to find out, was that Chiang Kai-shek had no intention of fighting the Japanese. For a while, the United States flirted with the Chinese Communists, hoping that perhaps they might be persuaded to take on the Japanese army on the mainland, but the fact was that neither the Nationalists nor the Communists intended to make a major effort to raise and train the troops to fight the Japanese. Their attention was focused elsewhere—on each other and the future control of China. When the American authorities finally realized they could not rely on the Nationalist Chinese or on Chiang Kei-shek to take on the Japanese army when the time came for an Allied invasion of the Japanese home islands, they began to search for other ways of achieving this aim.

The choice finally made was to invite Russia to pin down the Japanese forces on the mainland during the final phase of the war. Since the Soviet Union was not at war with Japan, this raised the large question of Soviet intervention in the war as well as the timing for such invention. At Yalta, Russia's role was formally recognized by the agreement which Roosevelt signed with Stalin giving the Russians certain concessions (called by some the Great Betrayal) in return for Stalin's promise to enter the war against Japan three months after the defeat of Germany and at a time when we were ready to land troops on Japan. This was an agreement which MacArthur, Nimitz and the Joint Chiefs of Staff recommended strongly and repeatedly. It is not at all evident, as Professor Iriye believes, that this agreement was designed to make the United States supreme in the Far East. Rather, it would seem that the agreement reached at Yalta achieved more in the long run for the Soviet Union than it did for the United States.

There has been considerable controversy in the postwar period over the Yalta Agreement. The two naval members of the Joint Chiefs of Staff, Admirals Leahy and King, accepted the necessity for Soviet intervention reluctantly but could find no way to avoid it and the concommitant price that had to be paid Stalin. In their postwar memoirs both claimed that the United States did not need Russia in the war at all. As a matter of fact, by 1945 it did not, but negotiations for intervention had gone so far down the road that the Americans could not very well break them off. Nor could they prevent the Russians from entering the war against Japan and moving troops into the area if the Russians chose to do so. Much of this reasoning lies behind the thesis that the United States used the atomic bomb primarily to end the war before the Soviet Union could intervene, thus securing a voice in the postwar settlement in the Far East. The Soviets declared war on August 9, the same day that the second bomb was dropped on Nagasaki. The war ended soon thereafter; whether as a result of the bombing or Soviet intervention is still an open question. Professor Iriye's picture of a postwar power structure in the Far East based on the Yalta Agreement, therefore, would seem to require modification. And even if he is correct, and the United States sought to use the war as an opportunity to secure domination in the Far East, the plan failed. By 1949, the Nationalist regime of Chiang Kai-shek had been driven from the mainland, and soon thereafter the occupation of Japan came to an end. The French were driven from Southeast Asia by 1954, and the United States, despite the longest and most bitter war in its history, has also finally withdrawn from the area.

Part III

Trade and Investment Patterns and Economic Policies in the Pacific

Chapter Ten

Introduction

Kenneth J. Rothwell

The world is groping for new relationships in international economic affairs, particularly in such areas as currency, trade and investment, and foreign aid. The economic issues which emerge from new political realities facing Pacific countries are created partly by the complexity of economic relationships involving trade, investment, aid and world resources, and partly by the diversity of economic participants in the region itself. Trade, finance, employment, output and economic growth have divergent trends in different parts of the Pacific region. Dynamic transformation proceeds alongside traditional conservatism; and economic concentration is frequently ringed with economic sparcity and isolation. Some of the fastest-growing as well as the slowest-growing economies are to be found in the Pacific area.

The Pacific Basin is a vast geographical area containing large and minute land masses with enormous diversities in national wealth and resources, levels of per capita GNP, rates of economic change, and economic impact. There are at least thirty countries in or ringing the Pacific with populations in excess of two million people. Almost one-half of the world's population live in countries touching the Pacific. There are thousands of islands uninhabited or with a handful of individuals along with giant land masses under- and overpopulated. The Pacific Basin includes countries with long and short national identities. Cultural, historical and social relationships present no consistent pattern. Nevertheless, an attempt to show some common economic characteristics of the various nations of the Pacific Basin is given in Table 10–1. It is not possible in this review to state the full range of economic variation; instead we will focus only on the peaks of economic achievement or on the glaring disparities of economic breakthrough or dysfunction.

Table 10–1. Nations of the Pacific: Selected Economic Data

Country (Ranked by Population Within Region)	Population (1972) (m)	GNP per Capita (1972) ($)	Exports FOB (1973) ($b)	Public Expenditures (per Capita)			Foreign Aid	
				Military ($)	(1971) Education ($)	Health ($)	Given (1971) ($m)	Received (1971) ($m)
Asia[a]								
China	836	144	—	12	7	—	75	—
U.S.S.R.	248	1,790	—	268	158	69	400	—
Indonesia	126	80	3.1	2	—	—	1,484	546
Japan	107	2,750	37.0	45	75	4	1,484	—
Philippines	41	195	1.8	3	7	2	—	189
Thailand	40	183	1.6	6	6	1	—	172
Republic of Korea	33	274	3.2	11	11	1	—	391
North Vietnam	21	100	—	15	5	1	—	—
South Vietnam	19	200	—	59	3	1	—	438
Taiwan	15	451	4.4	33	14	1	—	110
North Korea	14	330	—	49	10	1	—	—
Malaysia	11	394	3.0	17	19	6	—	64
Cambodia	7	110	—	18	5	1	—	19
Hong Kong	4	—	5.0	—	—	—	—	—
Singapore	2	—	3.6	—	—	—	—	—
South America								
Colombia	23	328	1.5	5	11	6	—	257
Peru	14	493	1.0	14	15	5	—	110
Chile	10	796	1.2	18	42	20	—	181
Ecuador	7	260	.6	4	13	1	—	27
North and Central America								
U.S.A.	209	5,510	71.3	379	264	130	3,903	—
Mexico	53	670	2.6	4	16	8	—	300
Canada	22	4,760	25.9	89	325	133	422	—
Guatemala	5	360	.4	5	6	4	—	28

El Salvador	4	300	.4	3	11	5	—	17
Honduras	3	280	.2	3	8	2	—	31
Nicaragua	2	430	.3	6	12	4	—	33
Costa Rica	2	560	.3	—	28	15	—	23
Panama	2	730	.1	1	36	14	—	33
Oceania[b]								
Australia	13	3,420	9.6	106	112	69	210	—
New Zealand	3	3,000	2.6	38	88	87	—	—
Papua New Guinea	2	300	—	—	—	—	—	—
Other Oceania	2	700	—	—	—	—	—	—

Notes: Data are for years indicated with minor exceptions.

a. Other Pacific nations of Asia not listed are: Ryuku Islands, Macao, Brunei. Population cutoff point is approximately two million.

b. Other Pacific nations not listed are: Portuguese Timor, Fiji Islands, British Solomon Islands, Western Samoa, French Polynesia, Guam, New Caledonia, Trust Territory of the Pacific Islands, Tonga, New Hebrides, Gilbert and Ellice Islands, American Samoa. Population cutoff point is approximately 2.5 million.

Sources: Data are derived from the following:

"World Bank Atlas–Population, Per Capita Production and Growth Rates," *Finance and Development Quarterly*, IMF and IBRD, Washington, D.C., vol. no. 1, March 1972;

World Military Expenditures 1971, U.S. Arms Control and Disarmament Agency, Washington, D.C.;

International Financial Statistics, September 1974, IMF, Washington, D.C.;

Development Cooperation–1973 Review, OECD, Paris, 1973;

Trends in Developing Countries, World Bank Group: IBRD, 1973.

THE PACIFIC BASIN AS AN ECONOMIC REGION

As was demonstrated in World War II and up to the end of the Vietnam War, the Pacific Basin has been more a strategic area where fundamental conflicts are played out rather than a unified economic entity forging ahead on a recognized front. Future economic performance will be governed more by the economic programs of one or two chief actors than by common policies involving a majority of the economies of the region. Although there has been much talk of a Pacific Free Trade Area, its operational emergence seems unlikely in the near future. Its economic formation tends to be largely a response to critical regional unifications elsewhere. For example, the reaction to the strength of the European Economic Community can be seen in regional reconstructions in various parts of the world, including the Pacific grouping. A Pacific Free Trade Area is, of course, more likely than an Atlantic Free Trade Area and clearly would be a less attractive alternative than any movement toward genuine global and multilateral free trade. Such an area may have possibilities for limited groups of countries in the region. These, however, are multinational groupings with special interests, such as in particular commodities, rather than regional geographical groupings of countries. The reason for this incompleteness of concern is that some Pacific countries are as much identified with other groups in the world as by Pacific Ocean concerns. In general, oceans do not seem to be as strong a unifying force as contiguous land masses. On the other hand, some elements in the basin are almost exclusively contained by the events in the basin region.

In the absence of formal or official regional organizations or political relationships, the trend toward a Pacific unification will be fostered instead, but to a lesser degree and on a more narrow basis, by the roles of the multinational corporations. Essentially, these institutions bring development without local control and economic change without local participation. A country's access to international capital is widened and its natural resources are made accessible to a world economic community. In this sense, the economic resources of the world are made more freely available although employment opportunities and income equities may not be maintained.

The mutuality of interests of trading partners of Pacific countries is not always a viable prospect, because trading barriers and the emergence of neomercantilism offset the advantages which would otherwise accrue. These distortions and restrictions of commodity trade in the region impose losses of real income on poor countries in the region. Prospects of increased protectionism in the United States, some slowing down of the regional integration in Europe, and the role of the U.S.–Soviet Union detente and expanding relationships with China divert traditional trading patterns, especially under conditions of declining interest in foreign aid. This means that the trading activities of Pacific countries will have to be sustained chiefly by the Pacific countries themselves. Worldwide inflation and the oil emergency have made the plight of some developing countries in the region of crisis proportions. Population pressures add to the burdens of some members of the region and then disproportionately to the land area available. The rise in export potentials promised through the Green Revolution has not materialized. The prospects for trade liberalization of benefit to the Pacific nations do not seem hopeful.

TRADE PATTERNS IN THE PACIFIC

Trade and investment are two elements of critical concern in judging performance and capabilities of the international community. Exchanges between Pacific area partners has increased significantly over the past several years. Foremost in the thrust of change has been the new structures of trade and investment forced on the area by the extraordinary growth of Japan. Total exports from Japan are now more than half the United States total, but in respect to exports to Pacific nations the Japanese figure is equal in amount to that of the United States.

Table 10–2 shows a trade matrix for Pacific area countries for 1973. Both conceptually and statistically, this matrix presents many difficulties. For example, the trade between the United States and Canada—even though both are Pacific nations—cannot really be treated as intra-Pacific trade. To overcome this difficulty, the figures have been based upon an assumption that 25 percent of United States trade with Canada can be ascribed to the Pacific side of these countries' relationships. A similar assumption is made with respect to trade between Mexico, the United States and Canada. The U.S.S.R. is a major Pacific nation but statistics useful for contributing to a trade matrix are not readily available. Furthermore, because of the innumerable small nations, it is not possible to present a complete matrix of all Pacific trade.

Nevertheless, from the figures presented in the matrix, it can be said that about one-half of all world trade is between Pacific nations. Of this intra-Pacific trade, the United States and Japan are the giants. Two-thirds of the total trade of Pacific nations is with partners in the Pacific region. This regionalization has been increasing steadily since the early 1950s.

Japan exported to Pacific partners about $23 billion in 1973, which is about the same as United States Pacific exports. But these Japanese exports represent 61 percent of its total exports whereas they are only 32 percent for the U.S. These volumes of intra-Pacific trade are three to four times that of the next largest trading partners—Australia and Canada. Hong Kong, Taiwan and Singapore are the next group of Pacific country traders, with between $2 and $3 billion of exports each. Mainland China's trade with the United States, which amounted to $92 million in 1972—the first full year after the lifting of U.S. embargoes, rose to about $657 million in 1973 and was expected to rise another 40–60 percent in 1974. U.S.S.R. exports to the United States amounting to $96 million in 1972 rose to $214 million in 1973 and to about $400 million in 1974. U.S. exports to the U.S.S.R., on the other hand, were more than double their

Table 10–2.   Intra-Pacific Area Trade Matrix—1973[a] *($ million)*

EXPORTS TO[c] FROM → ↓	U.S.A.[b]	Japan	Canada[b]	Australia	Hong Kong
U.S.A.[b]	–	9,561	4,260	1,088	1,414
Japan	8,344	–	1,689	3,011	486
Canada[b]	3,770	1,000	–	214	109
Australia	1,443	1,196	203	–	176
Hong Kong	740	1,119	28	150	–
Taiwan	1,168	1,644	31	99	207
Singapore	684	931	15	207	247
New Zealand	247	267	47	529	41
Malaysia	162	448	30	157	62
Mexico[b]	834	191	27	17	9
Philippines	495	621	24	67	33
Peru	415	141	47	4	2
Indonesia	441	904	14	122	139
China (Mainland)	657	1,041	289	124	53
Other Pacific Countries	3,577	3,562	192	187	238
Total Pacific Countries	22,977	22,626	6,896	5,976	3,216
(Percent of total exports)	(32)	(61)	(29)	(86)	(64)

Notes:

a. Values of exports for most countries have been estimated from incomplete annual data.

b. Because trade between these countries can be across contiguous land borders, or can be as much associated with Atlantic trade as Pacific trade, intercountry Pacific trade has been estimated on the basis of 25 percent of total intercountry trade.

c. Countries are listed in rank order of total exports. In some cases estimates are made from information on source of imports rather than distribution of exports.

Source: Derived from IMF *Direction of Trade,* Monthly.

imports from the U.S.S.R. However, it is not possible to claim all of this trade as trans-Pacific.

Some countries are only incidentally Pacific trading countries; others are almost wholly Pacific-oriented in their exports. For example, Indonesia and the Philippines each export over 90 percent of all exports to other Pacific countries. The Table 10–3 shows the degree of the orientation of export trade within the Pacific nations.

INVESTMENT DEVELOPMENTS

There have been several distinct generations of foreign investment activity in the Pacific. The region was a distant outpost for much of traditional colonial investment, but a vital area of imperialist competition. Thus Dutch and British interests as well as French, Portuguese, Spanish and German clashed on

Table 10-2. (cont.)

Taiwan	Singapore	New Zealand	Malaysia	Mexico[b]	Philippines	Peru	Indonesia
1,669	556	409	302	286	663	338	252
815	244	417	474	74	822	145	1,020
169	30	66	44	4	17	8	3
99	110	153	52	9	15	2	40
289	154	26	50	1	26	–	10
–	36	14	32	5	52	2	95
121	–	19	548	1	11	1	197
5	20	–	10	4	–	–	1
31	582	34	–	–	4	–	51
5	12	1	2	–	–	15	–
28	16	25	20	1	–	2	1
1	2	35	1	14	–	–	–
117	96	–	16	–	5	–	–
–	42	3	60	9	4	46	–
163	244	68	86	36	53	33	56
3,512	2,144	1,270	1,697	444	1,672	592	1,726
(89)	(70)	(47)	(69)	(19)	(94)	(57)	(95)

numerous occasions up to 1914. United States interests emerged more distincly and exclusively after World War I, adding to the extent of foreign control. Japanese interests spread throughout the Pacific with increasing intensity up to 1941, when economic measures gave way to widespread military exploits which, being unsuccessful, eventually resulted in severe contractions in its economic sphere of influence. The ending of colonial dominance was replaced, first by private international investment originating mainly from the United States and then, in the late 1960s, by large amounts from Japan; and, second, by the complex multinational type of investment. Extraction of natural resources has been the overriding objective of much of this investment, although the creation of great trading and manufacturing centers such as Singapore, Hong Kong and Taiwan has also been accomplished in this phase.

Investment potentials in the seventies for the Pacific nations will be dominated by Japanese capabilities. In 1972, for example, Japanese overseas private investments were almost four times that of the previous year. The total overseas claims at the end of 1972 had been built up within a very short period of time. In 1973, overseas assets, particularly short-term, increased by about 100 percent. By the end of 1972, Japan had made overseas private investments totalling $6.8 billion. The structure of this accumulation of overseas investments is shown in Table 10-4. Of this total, Asia accounted for 21 percent, Oceania 6

Table 10–3.   Pacific-Oriented Trade—1973

	Value of exports (U.S. $b.)	*Percent of all exports*
Indonesia	1.7	95
Philippines	1.7	94
Taiwan	3.5	89
Australia	6.0	86
Singapore	2.1	70
Malaysia	1.7	69
Hong Kong	3.2	64
Japan	22.6	61
Peru	.6	57
New Zealand	1.3	47
U.S.A.	23.0	32
Canada	6.9	29
Mexico	.4	19

Table 10–4.   Japan's Private Overseas Investments—1972

	(U.S. $ billion)
Acquisition of securities	3.6
Loans	2.4
Acquisition of real estate and direct overseas investments	.5
Overseas branches	.3
Total:	6.8

percent, North America 23 percent and Latin America 15 percent. Most was in mining industries, followed by finance and insurance industries.

This pattern of investment suggests some of the newer elements of overall Pacific Basin investment trends: the creation of financial centers and capital markets increasingly independent of the traditional centers in London, New York and European capitals. The Asian currency market or the Asian dollar market emerged in Singapore following the rapid growth of the Eurocurrency market. Asian Currency Units are used by a growing number of banks authorized by the Monetary Authority of Singapore. Thus the region is becoming increasingly sophisticated and capable of generating its own savings for the needed investments for future decades. Again, Japanese financial contributions are likely to be the most significant, even including United States sources. Questions of freedom of entry to foreign investment and full national treatment of foreign firms will be critical in shaping investment trends for the rest of the 1970s.

FOREIGN AID

The total volume of official development assistance in real terms has been stagnant for most countries in recent years. The contributions of both Japan and the United States are far below the target of 0.7 percent of GNP adopted at the third meeting of the United Nations Conference on Trade and Development. Contributions from both countries have declined markedly as a proportion of GNP: in 1972 it was only 0.3 percent.

For some countries in the Pacific, Japanese aid is far more prominent than United States aid, although overall aid from the United States amounts to double that from Japan. The U.S.S.R. and Canada are the next largest suppliers of aid of all countries fringing the Pacific. Major recipients of aid in the region in order of receipts (1971) are shown in Table 10–5.

It would seem desirable that both common defense and aid to developing countries should be joint responsibilities of countries economically capable of making the contributions. Defense expenditures in Japan are less than 1 percent of GNP compared with 6 percent for the United States, suggesting that Japanese capabilities for social and economic development of the low income countries are much larger than is currently being undertaken. On a per capita basis, Japan spends far more on education than it does on the military, both being much less than foreign aid given. Table 10–6 compares the per capita aid expenditures against the military and education effort for the major aid donors in the Pacific region.

From this data it can be seen that the military and foreign aid effort for Japan takes second place to its concern for education. In Canada, however, which has growing foreign aid interests, the expenditure for education is also much greater than its military and foreign aid expenditure.

While the quality and quantity of foreign aid can be substantially improved in the years ahead, reference to domestic military and educational needs may not be as significant as reference to the economic and social development needs and capacity for absorption of low income countries. There are

Table 10–5. Major Pacific Aid Recipients—1971
(in order of receipts)

Indonesia	$546 million
South Vietnam	438
Republic of Korea	391
Mexico	300
Colombia	257
Philippines	189

Table 10–6. Per Capita Expenditures—1971 *(U.S. $)*

	Foreign Aid	*Military*	*Education*
U.S.A.	19	379	264
Japan	15	45	75
U.S.S.R.	2	268	158
Canada	19	89	325
Australia	16	106	112

growing needs for official international transfers among Pacific countries; hence the form that it takes and the principles under which it is made available will be of great consequence in the next decade.

CONCLUSIONS

The trade and investment issues which will plague the 1970s depend upon the course of the present world economic crisis, which is manifest chiefly in global inflationary forces and critical resource shortages. There is some threat that these forces will reduce levels of real income and output and engender nationalism or neomercantilism on a greater scale than was experienced in the 1930s. Fortunately, these threats do not seem to be well sustained at present, but some evidence of a cutback in investment flows, a drying up of foreign aid and policies of neomercantilism exacerbate the dangers.

The levels of change which were apparent in the beginning of the 1970s do not seem sustainable in the middle part of the decade, but the hope is that by the end of the decade the vigorous forces of economic change will have been resuscitated and will dispel the problems of excessive price change and intolerable levels of unemployment.

Although the problems of inflation and oil shortages are worldwide, there is little reason to suppose that these problems are more critical for Pacific nations than for other massive regions of the world. The pattern of resource distribution and the general conditions of interdependence in the Pacific area are quite dissimilar from those, say, of Africa, so that the political and exchange relationships between nations have different dimensions. Problems of food are certainly of much greater significance than problems of energy when comparing Pacific countries with the industrialized countries. The test of dealing with population pressures on available food supplies, therefore, will be of enormous concern. The Pacific nations with economic and political activities demonstrating greater degrees of complementarity will have a world economic role in the 1970s vastly different from any previous decade.

REFERENCES

Papers and Proceedings of the First Conference on Pacific Trade and Development. Tokyo, Japan: Economic Research Center, 1968.

H. E. English and Keith A. J. Hay. *Obstacles to Trade in the Pacific Area.* Proceedings of the Fourth Pacific Trade and Development Conference, Carleton University, Ottawa, Canada, 1972.

Harald B. Malmgren. *Pacific Basin Development: The American Interests.* Lexington, Massachusetts: D. C. Heath & Company, 1972.

Kiyoshi Kohima. *Japan and a Pacific Free Trade Area.* London: Macmillan, 1971.

———, "A Pacific Free Trade Area: A New Design for World Trade Expansion," *Hitotsubashi Journal of Economics,* June, 1971.

Asian Development Bank. *Southeast Asia's Economy in the 1970s.* London: Longmans Green & Co., Ltd., 1971.

N. W. Klatt. "Reflections on Agricultural Modernization in Asia." *Pacific Affairs* 46, no. 4 (Winter 1973–74): 534–547.

Allen Taylor. *Perspectives on U.S.–Japan Economic Relations.* Cambridge, Massachusetts: Ballinger Publishing Co., 1973.

Harry A. Cahill. *The China Trade and U.S. Tariffs.* New York: Praeger Publishers, 1973.

Donald R. Sherk. *The United States and the Pacific Trade Basin.* San Francisco: Federal Reserve Bank of San Francisco, 1970.

Chapter Eleven

Pacific Economic Potentials and Policies

H. Edward English

The Pacific economic stage is "where the action is" now and probably will be for the remainder of this century. This is true in two senses: (1) some Pacific area countries already enjoy among the highest economic growth rates, and others are exhibiting the potential to join the leaders; and (2) the relationships among Pacific area countries are fluid, and the potential for new economic partnerships or regional arrangements boggles the imagination.

Perhaps, as the more cautious or pessimistic will claim, the Pacific is too big or too heterogeneous to be considered a region where constructive cooperative arrangements can emerge. Undoubtedly Pacific arrangements will fall short of comprehensive regional groups such as the European Community. (But it is partly because the European Community exists that initiatives for Pacific partnerships or groups may eventually receive high priority.)

Let us pause for a minute to list the dramatis personae on the Pacific stage. There are essentially three principal types of actors: (1) the two great economic powers—the United States and Japan; (2) the minor wealthy countries—Canada, Australia and New Zealand; and (3) the two groups of poorer countries—those of Latin America and those of East and Southeast Asia. Then there are the offstage powers whose presence motivates the main actors, but who may not appear directly in the main play—the Eurasian economic and political powers, the EEC and the Soviet Union; and the mainly political giants, China and India.

The various scenarios that can be written using these actors will all demand major roles for the United States and Japan, but what kind of roles? It is entirely possible that both will play so passive a role as to make the play a tedious account of reactions to offstage forces. Or, the major actors can be individual or joint initiatives challenge the offstage powers to respond to the dynamism of their policies and achievements. The lesser actors must be ready to react to a variety of stimuli from the leads, and to seize opportunities to guide Pacific affairs in directions that serve their interests.

The ingredients of Pacific economic relationships are monetary policy, commercial policy and development finance (investment and foreign aid). Another factor that affects the relationships among the Pacific area countries—security arrangements—has been important in the past, but it is in no small part because of the decline in importance of those arrangements that economic factors are becoming paramount. Let us focus on each of the three ingredients of economic relationships in order to define their character and then discuss briefly each actor and his probable role.

First, the monetary issue, which I shall dispose of quickly, although not because it is unimportant. It could be so important as to frustrate any and all efforts at constructive Pacific cooperation. But I think not. The history of postwar international monetary relationships, in spite of frequent failure to face realities, has nevertheless revealed a willingness to change. No nation has been so tenacious about its own monetary "ideology" as to refuse to accept substantial changes in the value of its own currency. I think this is because, however unwelcome such policies as revaluation appear in the short run, they do involve moderate change, with burdens being shared widely in the economy. The United States, which has had to acknowledge the greatest shift in its currency's role has, albeit rather belatedly, accepted the consequences and begun to adapt both itself and the system. Japan, too, has given up its resistance to change, and has accepted a massive revaluation in two steps and even a temporarily flexible exchange rate. Clearly, so long as more fundamental economic interests can be protected, countries will accept monetary reform. Many still say that this is an unreasonably optimistic view, that the 1930s provide contradictory evidence of what can happen. However, policymakers now better understand the origins of international monetary crises—the need for adequate liquidity arrangements, and in recent years even the importance of controlled exchange rate adjustment as a means of adapting to differing growth rates and avoiding unacceptable inflationary pressures. In any case, in the present context it must be stressed that the world's monetary problems will not be solved except by arrangements that involve all the major economic powers. The Pacific area countries by themselves can do little except to come to a common understanding of the parameters of an effective monetary system.

The direction of trade and development policies involves both greater uncertainty and many more challenging issues in Pacific area relationships. The economic and political interests that trade and capital flows can serve do not require the virtual universality of participation that monetary policies may necessitate. The choice between the multilateral and regional approach can be a pragmatic one. Which type of arrangement is feasible or available at any time? Can regional schemes achieve some of the major objectives of multilateral arrangements, and even contribute to the realization of multilateral aims?

In the Pacific area, the major economic powers, Japan and the United States, have had a strong multilateral bias. The United States has had too many political interests internationally (especially since World War II) to take a narrow regional approach to any of its relationships; Japan has been reluctant to rely on its relationships within the East and Southeast Asian region. This is due in part to the failure of its aggressive policies in the 1930s and 1940s, and the markedly different ideologies and the degree of continental self-sufficiency of its two major continental neighbours in Asia. But there is another more fundamental reason why Japan has come to regard its worldwide relationships as essential to its economic success. The role of North America and Western Europe in world trade is of overwhelming importance, and only markets of this size and complexity are sufficient to accommodate the Japanese, since their GNP approximately equals that of all South and East Asia, including China and India.

There can thus be no doubt that whatever international economic relationships emerge during the next few years, these arrangements will be unsatisfactory to both Japan and the United States if they hamper the prospects for expanding trade with Europe. This does not mean, of course, that Pacific regional initiatives are excluded. It means that such initiatives should not be protectionist or exclusive in implication. They should either promote liberalization of trade with Europe or be neutral. It becomes essential then to define areas of substantial common interest in the Pacific region and to identify the effect of the pursuit of these common interests upon negotiations with Europe.

Against the background of these considerations, let us examine in turn the economic interests and attitudes of each of the major Pacific area countries and groups.

JAPAN

Japanese future interests and attitudes are in some ways easier to define than those of any other major trading country. This is in part because Japan's international needs and potentialities as well as her limitations are easier to define than those of North America or Western Europe. But it is also because the Japanese give every indication of responding to perceived future requirements in a more rational way than we do in North America.

> The view is widespread that in the 1970s Japan will have such problems as inflation and environmental disruption internally and will face mounting tensions in its trade and economic relations with other areas externally, as its economic strength increases. In order to solve these internal and external problems, Japan will need to promote and maintain free trade.

I believe this is a correct assessment and that the Japanese government will act quickly. My conviction is reenforced by the recent experience of the adoption of a flexible rate for the yen, a radical departure for the Japanese government.

According to the outlook reported in *Japan's Economy in 1980 in the Global Context,* the Japan Economic Research Centre expects that Japan's share of world GNP will rise to 12.5 percent from about half that level in 1970. The Japanese expect that the EEC share will rise from 15.5 percent to 16.4 percent of world GNP in the same period, and that the U.S. share will decline from 32.1 percent to 25.3 percent.[1] Expectations regarding exports are a little less dramatic. The Japanese share is expected to increase from 6.2 to 10.8 percent, while the U.S. share will remain steady at 13.7 percent and the EEC will go from 28.4 to 29.6 percent.[2]

The changes expected in the composition of Japanese trade indicate a striking shift to more complex manufactures—heavy industrial goods, including chemicals, machinery and other metal manufactures—are shown in Table 11–1.

An interesting additional statistic is that for primary iron and steel products, which were 9.1 percent of total exports in 1960, grew to 14.7 percent in 1970, but are expected to fall to 8.8 percent in 1980. This reflects the recognition that, with Japan's resource shortage, the upgrading of imported raw materials using her "plentiful" skilled labor and management is the soundest basic for exports. The relative rise in primary iron and steel products was a temporary phenomenon.

The directional pattern in Japanese trade as shown in Table 11–2 indicates their hopes for increased sales in markets they have not as effectively penetrated. Western Europe and the planned economies are expected to take 27.8 percent of Japan's exports and supply 25.2 percent of her imports in 1980, up from about 20 percent in 1970. However, North America and Asia will continue as Japan's largest trading partners, accounting for 58.2 percent of her exports and 57.2 percent of her imports (down from 62 to 63 percent in 1970). Japanese forecasters are taking account of the resistance in North America to Japanese exports and the necessity of increasing imports to increase their prospects for market penetration in Europe and sustain their positions in North America and Southeast Asia. Nevertheless, they forecast a $6 billion positive trade balance vis-à-vis North America and a similar balance with Europe. Only

Table 11–1.   Japanese Exports—1960, 1970, 1980 *(percent)*

	1960	*1970*	*1980*
Food and raw materials	8.2	4.4	1.8
Light industrial goods (textiles, etc.)	48.4	22.4	11.9
Heavy industrial goods	43.4	72.4	86.3
Chemicals	4.2	6.4	7.4
Machinery	25.4	46.3	65.8
Electrical	6.8	14.8	20.8
Transport	10.7	17.8	22.4

Table 11–2. Japanese Trading Patterns—1960, 1970, 1980 *(percent)*

	1960		1970		1980	
	Exports	*Imports*	*Exports*	*Imports*	*Exports*	*Imports*
North America	30.4	42.7	34.1	34.5	32.4	31.4
Western Europe	11.7	9.3	15.1	10.9	19.2	15.5
Asia	35.7	27.4	28.0	28.4	25.8	25.8
Australia, New Zealand and South Africa	5.6	9.6	5.5	10.4	5.5	9.5
Latin America	6.8	6.2	5.1	6.5	3.5	4.0
Planned economies	1.8	2.8	5.4	4.9	8.6	9.7

with one group of countries, Australia, New Zealand and South Africa, do they anticipate a trade deficit. They are worried about the size of these surpluses, but believe that it is reasonable to expect Japanese outpayments on invisibles and capital and aid to act as a counterbalance. Clearly they have underestimated the pressure for a higher exchange value. The free rate has reached 260 yen per dollar, as compared with the 280 yen per dollar they forecast for 1980. They may also have underestimated the pressure for (and effect of) liberalization of Japanese imports, especially from Southeast Asia, and overestimated the willingness of Europeans to liberalize their import restraints on Japanese goods.

However, the policy directions are clear for Japan. They include:

1. cooperation with the United States in efforts to expand trade with Europe;
2. definite moves toward liberalization of Japan's tariffs and nontariff barriers, and controls on foreign investment; and
3. bilateral efforts to build trade with China and the Soviet bloc.

The last of these has the least direct bearing upon Japan's trade with the market economies. To the extent that it is successful, Japan's exports to the planned economies are likely to be competitive with North American capital goods exports, and her imports from China are likely to compete with those from Southeast Asia, while the Soviet Union will supply industrial materials, notably energy and forest products, in competition with Canada.

The other two major trading policy directions should ensure active Japanese cooperation in the next GATT round, including a willingness to liberalize Japan's trade in agricultural products (except for rice). In order to achieve the massive expansion of exports of advanced manufactures contemplated, Japan will have to convince North America and Europe that her domestic market for similar goods is no longer closed by substantial nontariff barriers. There have already been significant moves toward elimination of the more formal nontariff barriers and an increasingly clear commitment to reduction or elimination of tariffs in the "Nixon" round. But there remains a skepticism concerning Japan's intentions regarding her own peculiar (some would say notorious) forms of administrative control. To a degree, the restrictive effect of some of these controls is exaggerated; or so we are assured not only by official spokesmen but also by independent academic economists from Japan. But it is likely that both the fears (and the substance) regarding such practices will be modified only when foreign businesses have a fuller opportunity to operate in and from Japan. Thus, the nature and extent of liberalization of direct investment controls may be of crucial importance in any bargain between Japan and North America (and of increasing importance in dealings with Europe, to the extent that Europe shows any substantial interest in expanding trade with Japan).

A growing tension on trade relations between Japan and Southeast

Asia (and India) may be expected over the access to the Japanese market for light manufactures for which this region is becoming an increasingly competitive supplier. In this area, Japanese investment and aid, to be both acceptable and effective, must be accompanied by market access. In all its relations with this region, Japanese policymakers are sensitive to two aspects of the relationship:

1. their equivocal political reputation, dating from the days of the coprosperity sphere; and
2. the uncertain dimensions of the adjustment problem required to accommodate Southeast Asian exports if Japan were to become the most accessible market for such products.

Both of these considerations urge upon Japanese policymakers the desirability of joint trade and aid initiatives, involving other Pacific area developed countries, toward the Southeast and South Asian regions. It may be noted that while some of these features of Japanese policy interests have a direct bearing on the forthcoming GATT negotiations, many of them go well beyond the scope of any feasible GATT bargain. But more of this after the positions of the other Pacific countries have been reviewed.

THE UNITED STATES

It is presumptuous for me to say much about the trade expectations or policies of the United States in this company. Rather than to attempt anything parallel to the foregoing review of Japan's expectations, let me give an outsider's interpretation of U.S. trends. I have already mentioned the universality of U.S. political and economic interests, hence the tendency of postwar administrations to identify U.S. trade policies with multilateral institutions and initiatives. This attitude has contrasted sharply with U.S. practices in security, where regional arrangements have been the rule rather than the exception. Against this background, a number of observations about the future course of U.S. trade relations would appear justified.

The U.S. view of the future of world or Pacific trade involves no projection of major changes in the role of trade in the U.S. economy or of trade policy in U.S. foreign relations. In a recent paper, Lawrence Krause emphasizes that the United States has become a postindustrial economy with a heavy bias toward services.[3] He suggests that this means that trade will have a decreasing importance to many American producer groups. The notable (and ironic) exception may be agriculture. Another exception is the technologically intensive goods category. But while the United States will continue to play a role in this sector, the lead it has had over the past decade should continue to decline as other major trading countries respond with increasing effectiveness to the American challenge. Krause and others may place too little emphasis on the export of U.S. services, notably financial and managerial services, though there is in his paper (as in U.S. economic literature more generally) an acceptance of the proposition that the United States has a comparative advantage in the export of capital. It is not as clear that there is yet official acceptance of the related proposition that a substantial negative trade balance should be regarded as normal for the United States, as it was for Britain in the pre–World War II period.

Since the recent balance of payments preoccupation, the United States has emphasized the negative effect of other countries' trade policies upon U.S. export potentials. Attention was (correctly, I believe) first focused on exchange rates. The adjustment mechanism was clearly in need of attention. But when issues in trade policy were raised as a means of dealing with the so-called U.S. balance of payments problem, there was more risk that the real issues in trade policy would be misinterpreted or even neglected. It would always seem preferable that trade policies be evaluated on allocation grounds—do they contribute to or detract from an optimum national and international allocation of industrial activity?

In fact, U.S. trade policy in the Pacific seems likely to be based on a political interest in strengthening economic ties with Japan now that security arrangements have become a less important basis for a U.S. "presence" in that area. With Japan directly, the United States is sure to be interested not only in liberalization of agricultural trade (especially for products such as beef when and if supplies expand), but also in two-way trade in advanced manufactures. The latter can be pursued both through trade policy liberalization and through removal or reduction of Japanese investment controls. In turn, the United States must expect to temper its demands for voluntary export restraints. Furthermore, it may find it useful to show a positive attitude toward the acceptance of some of the economic demands of the developing countries, especially for access to U.S. and Japanese markets.

PACIFIC AREA DEVELOPING COUNTRIES

This last point opens up the question of focus between the major economic powers and the two groups of developing countries most closely associated with the United States and Japan—Latin America and East and Southeast Asia. Latin American trade comprises only 10 percent of U.S. trade, and Asia as a whole (except for Japan and the Communist countries) takes another 15 percent of U.S. exports and supplies about 8 percent of U.S. imports. These figures compare with those already quoted for Japan—6.5 percent for Latin America and about 26 percent for Asia. This comparison reveals the greater established trading capacity of Asia (a disproportionate share of which is accounted for by the most developed East Asian countries, Hong Kong, Taiwan and Korea). It also suggests very strongly that a great unused potential remains. During the next decade, the East Asian group and some of those in Southeast Asia will be capable of great expansion of export of light manufactures, and some Latin American countries will not be far behind, as the recent example of Brazil indicates. For these countries the improvement of access to the developed-country markets of the region will become a top priority. The Southeast Asian countries, with the "showcase" examples of Hong Kong and Singapore at hand, have become increasingly vocal on this issue, and Latin American trade policy specialists now recognize that export of manufactures can be vitally important in the identification and growth of leading sectors.

So far, the developing countries have relied heavily upon UNCTAD as the means for formulating and pressing their demands for market access. This has resulted in some refinement of concepts, but it has not brought significant real gains to the developing countries. The main reason is partly the cumbersomeness of an organization with so many members, but it is probably more fundamentally a question of the heterogeneity of the interests affected, and the lack of urgent concern on the part of the developed countries. These countries recognize that the existing trade flows affecting their export interests are those between developed countries, and apparently see no urgency in liberalizing trade on behalf of their consumers when the immediate direct cost to some labor-intensive sectors of the producing economy are more evident. It does not appear to matter, in the short run, that this myopia contributes to the frustration of development sectors having the greatest potential in the developing countries, or that it contributes to a growing cynicism about the commercial policies of developed countries and about the genuineness of their convictions concerning the merits of the market system in economic development.

The current aspect of these problems that receives a disproportionate share of attention is the preferences issue. The issue has been highlighted because of the priority placed on it by UNCTAD and by the policies of the European Economic Community. The Latin American countries in particular have been concerned about the preferred position which African goods experience in the EEC, and this concern has been heightened by the growing prospect of Caribbean countries receiving the same preferences. Furthermore, many Latin Americans are not particularly enthusiastic about the implication that they should seek out a parallel deal with the United States. For its part, the United States is unhappy about the preferences enjoyed by EEC goods in Africa.

The reason why all of this is a disproportionate emphasis is that the margins of preference contemplated are scarcely large enough to affect the directions of LDC trade, were the developing countries actually exploiting their labor-cost advantage. It is not the preferences themselves that are of paramount importance. The countries, especially the ex-colonial powers, that grant such preferences exercise administrative favoritism toward former colonies as a consequence of linguistic or legal convenience, personal associations, etc. Where the developing countries exploit these advantages, they are likely to be prime targets for quantitative controls or "voluntary" export restraints if they are unwise enough to succeed in expanding their export capability. How can the two major groups of Pacific area developing countries obtain assured access to developed-country markets, particularly when they are hesitant to commit themselves too exclusively to the designated "northern colossus" of their region? The obvious answer is that the two sides of the Pacific should join forces, at least in a trade and development strategy.

PACIFIC AREA SMALLER DEVELOPED COUNTRIES

Before exploring the specifics of the policy options, let us look briefly at the interests of the smaller developed countries. As a consequence of three factors, Australia and New Zealand have turned toward Asia quite naturally. The loss of special status in Britain has only reinforced and hastened the trade shift consequent on Japan's great leap forward in the 1960s and the major Australian mineral developments that have attracted so much attention in Japan. For these countries, Japan is soon to become the major trading partner. By 1980, the Japanese estimate that over 40 percent of Australia's and New Zealand's exports will go to Japan, twice the percentage in 1970. By comparison, the North American market is expected to absorb only about 11 percent of Japan's exports. This largely reflects the expected growth of industrial materials exports. But Japan also expects that it will supply about a third of Australia's and New Zealand's imports in 1980, as compared with less than half that fraction in 1970. Undoubtedly Japan feels it will be in a good position to press its manufactured exports on Australia and New Zealand because those countries (especially Australia) will have a uniquely large trade surplus with Japan. But expansion of trade with Japan faces two powerful obstacles so far as Australia and New Zealand are concerned. First, there is the question of access to Japan's market for their traditional agricultural products. In fact, except for lamb, the indications are increasingly positive that Japan will reduce its restrictions on the imports of these products. (Lamb is most doubtful mainly because it has not won consumer acceptance in Japan.) Its rising living standard promises an explosive increase in demand for beef and dairy products, and its own agriculture will be inadequate to meet this demand even if fully rationalized. The political problem of liberalization is much greater for rice than for livestock products.

The other problem is one that Australia and New Zealand share with Canada—the need to rationalize manufacturing by reducing infant industry protection that has long outlived its original purpose and has left manufacturing industries that are small scale and too diversified to be competitive internationally. The problem is accentuated in the Canadian case by the number of foreign firms that have entered the market in an effort to obtain market shares in Canada comparable to those they supply in the national market where the parent firm operates, usually the United States. In these circumstances, the liberalization of trade has a special purpose, the restructuring of industry so that each producer achieves the economies of firm and plant, and the dynamism that exposure of international competition is likely to instill.

Whatever the argument, it is clear that Canadians would generally be more enthusiastic about trading commitments that involve others besides the United States. This is the reason why they have traditionally favored multilateral GATT-type negotiations. But the difficulty with such negotiations at the present time is that they would not be really suited to Canadian needs unless they led to a firm and lasting commitment to free trade in manufactures, and at the same time permitted a set of transitional and rationalization policies that would ensure effective adaptation to competitive world market conditions.

An increasing number of applied economists concerned with industrial structure and trade problems are coming to the conclusion that a free trade area might be an essential ingredient of policy environment required to rationalize Canadian industry.

It is rumored that Canadian policymakers in recent months explored the possibility of special relationship with the European Community, but found little interest on the part of the European countries in associate members from North America. What about the Pacific? Clearly Japan is a willing trading partner, but are there terms that would suit Canada's national interests? Like Australia and New Zealand, Canada welcomes access to the Japanese market for industrial materials and even agricultural products. That market can and will provide scope for expanded Canadian production of minerals, forest products and agricultural commodities (including cereals, vegetable oils and livestock products). But it will provide increased scope for exported manufactured goods only on several conditions:

1. that Canadian industry is rationalized in the North American context sufficiently to make some Canadian final products capable of competing in the Japanese market; and
2. that Canadian firms are able to market, and in some instances produce, in Japan on equal terms to those afforded Japanese firms in Canada.

Both on economic and political terms, Canada, like the other smaller developed countries of the Pacific basin, has good reason for interest in the simultaneous liberalization of trade with the two economic superpowers of the Pacific region. Since, as suggested earlier, the developing countries of the region have a similar interest, there would appear to be a convergence of policy objectives. Can this be converted into a set of practical policy initiatives that might have some chance of acceptance by the superpowers and of succeeding once accepted?

The most obvious simplified model would be a free trade association in which the five developed economies would be virtual full members at the end of a transition period. The two large groups of developing countries might be afforded unilateral free access to the markets of the developed countries. Many modifications or variations on this model are of course possible, but certain features should be highlighted. The fact is that this policy should not really be considered a substitute for or second best option to the proposed GATT round. The better thought out and the more feasible a Pacific option becomes, the more likely it would be to promote the success of the next GATT round. On the other hand, any reasonable estimate of the outcome of those negotiations suggests that there will remain considerable scope for further commercial policy initiatives. It seems particularly likely that such commitments would need to provide wider scope for a rational pattern of trade in agricultural products, for the assurance of markets for the products of developing countries, and for the control of those nontariff practices that have significant impact on international trade.

A second point of vital importance is the impact of any Pacific area arrangement on the rest of the world and Western Europe in particular. It would of course be essential that any such initiatives not be aimed at embarrassing or excluding Europe, Africa or the rest of Asia. One of the primary aims of a Pacific arrangement would be to encourage those in Europe who wish to ensure that the community (and for that matter COMECON) should be outward-looking. Given political predilections of both the United States and Japan, it is inconceivable that the Pacific group would ever exclude European countries from any market they might seek to enter, or from any major mutual security or development aid commitment in Asia or Latin America in which it might wish to be involved.

The detailed internal characteristics of any practical Pacific area economic grouping would be much more complex and less tidy than the simple model suggests. For example:

1. So far as the U.S.–Japanese relationship is concerned, there might have to be elaborate transitional arrangements, and the final product is likely to fall short of a full free trade area. For example, a long phasing-in period might be provided in which the early stages might include commitments for the material reduction of nontariff barriers of particular importance for U.S.–Japan trade, with the later stages providing for reduction of formal trade barriers, through GATT negotiations, up to a date beyond which the elimination of barriers between Pacific countries could be effected by prearranged schedule. The nontariff barriers first eliminated might include the Japanese restrictions on direct investment and U.S. quantitative restrictions on Japanese products (including the "voluntary" restraints program).
2. So far as the unilateral free access for products from Latin America and Southeast Asia are concerned, again a phasing might be contemplated, with

some distinction being made between the timing and perhaps the scope of concessions to the poorest or least developed of the LDCs. There might also be negotiated limits to the levels of formal protection adopted by LDCs in exchange for the unilateral free trade offer by the developed countries of the region. In this way, developing countries would be encouraged to divert more resources into those export-oriented and import-competing sectors having the prospects for economic viability.

Essential to the arrangement made would be the avoidance of preferences offered by LDCs to the Pacific developed countries, and the assurance that concessions made to Latin American and Asian countries would be available on comparable terms, though perhaps with a modest time lag, to African and other nonmembers. This would ensure that both Europe and Africa would not suffer from the Pacific group. One might be hopeful that they could soon choose to negotiate the lowering of remaining barriers.

3. Finally, the smaller developed countries could in this context remedy their structural inefficiency problems and at the same time avoid too heavy dependency on any one of the economic superpowers. Even if the United States and Japan were unable to make the kind of commitments indicated under point 1, Canada might combine a free trade with the United States with a series of more specific deals with Japan that would expand prospects for trade in both raw materials and manufactures.

These observations on the characteristics of possible Pacific area trading arrangements suggest that such arrangements deserve close examination. It is likely that the main obstacles to effecting any such arrangement would lie in Washington, and for reasons that appear to relate more to a commitment to traditional attitudes and approaches to commercial policy than to an assessment of fundamental U.S. economic and political interests.

NOTES TO CHAPTER ELEVEN

1. The exchange rate assumed by 1980 was 280 yen to the $1 (35 percent below September 1971). It is already at about 260.
2. They expect that Soviet share of world GNP will be about 15 percent in 1980 and the Chinese 32 percent. These shares of world trade are 4.7 and .05 percent respectively.
3. Lawrence Krause, "The U.S. Economy and International Trade" (Paper delivered at the Fifth Pacific Trade and Development Conference, January, 1973).

Chapter Twelve

Foreign Investment in the Pacific: Trends and Policies

Donald R. Sherk

The shape and direction of the "new political economy in the Pacific" during the seventies will be influenced considerably by the private investment flows in the region. Yet, historically, policymakers have tended to overlook the importance of private investment in the overall mix of intercountry economic relationships, concentrating instead on trade, aid and payments considerations. In an earlier era this neglect might have been justified on the grounds that private investment, in its predominantly "portfolio" form, consti- tuted a simple resource transfer from source to recipient country. This justifica- tion has long since evaporated as foreign investment became "direct" investment and the chief investors became identified as multinational corporations.[1]

Especially now, as the nations of the Pacific begin to grapple with the complexities of Vietnam reconstruction and Asian regional development, the promises and problems of foreign investment must be placed high on the agenda. It seems reasonable, therefore, that a close examination of the Asian foreign investment trends and policies be undertaken. More specifically, the Asian investment experience of the region's two leading investing nations—the United States and Japan—will be examined, with particular attention given to invest- ment in manufacturing industries.[2]

U.S. AND JAPANESE DIRECT INVESTMENT: A GLOBAL VIEW

U.S. Direct Investment

The United States is the world's leading direct investor, accounting for approximately 60 percent of the total stock of foreign direct investment throughout the world. In 1946 the accumulated dollar value of U.S. direct investment abroad was $7.2 billion, an amount which was actually less than that recorded in 1929 ($7.5 billion). The flow of United States investment abroad began to accelerate in the late fifties, reaching a total of $32.8 billion by 1960. The decade of the sixties saw this figure grow by almost two and a half times, exceeding $78 billion by 1970, and the most recent official data available lists the total at the start of 1972 as $86 billion.[3]

In terms of geographical distribution, the postwar period witnessed a concomitant spreading out of the United States direct investment activity. In both 1929 and 1946, the Western Hemisphere accounted for over 75 percent of the total value. This figure has dropped constantly over the past two decades and in 1971 reached 46.3 percent. First Europe and then the rest of the world increased their relative shares. Europe's share of United States direct investment increased from 13.9 percent in 1946 to 32.1 percent in 1971, and the rest of the world (Asia, Africa and Oceania) increased its share from 8.3 percent to 21.6 percent over the same period.

The reasons for this fanning out of United States direct investment in the postwar period are several. Investment in Canada and, to a lesser extent, in Latin America, could be regarded as little different from domestic investment. Familiarity with customs, laws and language minimized the differences. As a result, these areas could be incorporated within decision-making horizons of U.S. companies with reasonable ease. With respect to extractive investments (the predominant prewar field), closeness to production sites, which reduced transportation costs and minimized uncertainty, was of paramount importance. As the industrial composition of U.S. direct investment shifted, nearness to the United States became less important. Finally, the postwar period saw the dissolution of the colonial systems of earlier years. As a result, the former colonial holdings of the European powers became more open to United States direct investment.

The growth of the manufacturing sector in the total United States foreign investment position has played an important role in promoting this geographical dispersion. The rapidly growing markets of Western Europe, together with the tariff policies followed by both the European Common Market and the European Free Trade Area, turned Europe into a magnet for United States investment. Once United States companies determined that operating across national borders was relatively easy they quite naturally enlarged their horizons to include the more distant continents. Revolutions in communications and air transport facilitated this geographical dispersion.

As they became experienced in operating abroad, more and more United States companies began to see themselves as companies of the world. In today's terminology, they became multinational corporations. As such, these companies were concerned not solely with market shares in the United States but with world market shares, and endeavored to match the investment thrusts of their competitors. Investments in manufacturing facilities abroad to produce and market final products became incorporated into a global production and distribution strategy of the parent firm. Such a strategy, often referred to as the internationalization of production, enabled manufactured inputs or component parts to be produced in one country, shipped to another country for assembly or further production, and finally sold in still other countries. The division of the production process into a series of discrete activities, located throughout the world according to costs of production, was the logical extension of companies first venturing abroad. It is largely this phenomenon which has led to a considerable expansion of United States direct investment in developing Asia. To these forces which have led to increased U.S. direct investment in developing Asia must be added the emergence of Japan as a major foreign investor.

Japanese Direct Investment

It was not until the sixties that Japan began to engage in foreign direct investment to any significant extent. In fact, through 1960 the accumulated total of Japanese direct investment abroad was less than $300 million. This is not surprising given the voracious domestic demand for capital to fuel Japan's rapid economic growth, and considering the precarious state of her balance of payments throughout the fifties.

Exchange restrictions were instituted by the Japanese government to strictly control both the amount and kinds of foreign investment allowed. Those foreign investment projects which received approval through the early sixties were designed to secure export markets, (e.g. foreign sales agencies) or to obtain vital raw materials, (e.g. Alaska pulp, Middle Eastern petroleum or Australian ore). By the late sixties an improved balance of payments, increased protectionism in major Japanese markets and rapidly rising Japanese wages combined to considerably expand Japanese foreign investment. By 1972 the accumulated value of Japanese investment was approximately $6 billion and of this amount nearly 60 percent had been registered in just three years, 1970–1972.

Projecting Japanese foreign direct investment over the remainder of the decade is a difficult exercise. But enough is known at present to be fairly confident about predicting an accumulated value by 1980 of between $25 and $30 billion. Is this approximately four- or five-fold increase over the decade realistic? I suggest that it is for several reasons.

To begin with, although there has been considerable liberalization in the exchange controls applied to Japanese foreign investment, restrictions remained in force into 1972. As recently as September of 1970 any proposed foreign investment project exceeding $300,000 had to receive the approval of both the Japanese Ministry of Finance and the Ministry of International Trade and Industry (MITI). Once the project was approved, the company or companies planning the project had then to petition another government agency for the necessary financing. Although this case by case administrative review is often reduced to little more than a formality, it has tended to act as a barrier to overseas investment.

Not only will the removal of control accelerate the out-flow of

Japanese overseas investment in the years to come, the dramatic improvement in the Japanese balance of payments will also add pressure in this direction. Throughout the last half of the sixties Japan's reserves of gold and foreign exchange remained in the $2 to $3.5 billion range, a meager margin of safety given the size of her annual trade. By the end of 1970 her reserves reached $4.4 billion, and then, in 1971 (the year of the "Nixon shocks"), skyrocketed to an amount in the region of $14 billion. An unofficial estimate in November of 1972 placed the value at $18.4 billion.

This rapid build-up of reserves stimulated a chorus of voices from abroad (and from some domestic sources) urging the upward revaluation of the yen. In order to reduce pressure for revaluation, the Japanese instituted an eight point crash program designed to curb the accumulation of reserves. One point of this program called for a vigorous effort to step up overseas investment.

Under pressure from the United States, the Japanese agreed in December of 1971 to up-value the yen by nearly 17 percent as part of the Smithsonian Agreement. The continued growth in reserves in 1972 and the surge of speculation in the world money markets led to another upward revaluation in February of 1973 by approximately 18 percent. The momentum for expanded overseas investment is increased as the yen price of foreign assets is reduced.

What portion of this greatly increased outflow of Japanese direct investment will go to developing Asia is also problematical. Asia's share of Japan's total overseas investment has been rising (31 percent in 1969), and an estimate of 25 percent by 1980 seems conservative. That would mean that between $6 and $7 billion of Japanese investment should be in place in developing Asia in 1980. Such an amount should match, if not surpass, the projected United States investment position in the region.

INVESTMENT PROFILES OF JAPAN AND THE UNITED STATES IN DEVELOPING ASIA

The Second World War marked a dramatic break in the political economy of most Asian nations. Prior to the war these states were colonies in European-based colonial systems. Britain with its Empire, France with Indochina and the Netherlands with East Indies all intermeshed their respective colonies into fairly rigid trade and investment systems so that the colonies became largely extensions of the mother country's economy. The Asian countries not included in these European colonial systems were not independent. The Philippines represented a U.S. brand of colonialism; Taiwan and Korea were vassals of Japan; Thailand, although formally independent was tied to Britain.

The war saw the colonial powers driven from the region by Japan, and the seeds of independence were sown. After the defeat of Japan, attempts by European powers to resume colonial control were thwarted and a wave of independence ensued throughout Asia. Almost all the newly independent states embarked upon industrial development drives and re-established economic ties with their former rulers. But for the most part the influence and presence of the European powers in Asia have waned. Although Britain's stake in Asia remains important, the region has increasingly become dominated by the economic power of the United States and, more recently, Japan.

Over the last ten years Asia has grown in importance in terms of total United States foreign direct investment, yet it remains behind Europe, Canada and Latin America. As a percent of total United States direct investment, Asia's share has increased from 3.4 percent in 1959 to 5.7 percent in 1971, its largest share in the postwar period. The figure, however, includes Japan; excluding Japan, developing Asia's share has risen from 2.5 percent in 1962 to 3.5 percent in 1971. Preliminary estimates for 1972 show this percentage being considerable higher, possibly as high as 4 percent. This contrasts markedly with the importance of developing Asia in the total for Japan, where the figure has been closer to one-fourth of the total.

In terms of industrial composition Japan has a larger share of its total invested in the manufacturing sector of developing Asia than does the United States, nearly 44 percent for Japan and 28 percent for the U.S. The U.S. has a larger share invested in petroleum than does Japan but trails Japan in the mining and smelting area.

However, these aggregate percentages mask important differences in the industrial composition of U.S. and Japanese investment in developing Asia as a whole and within individual Asian countries. In manufacturing, the Japanese have invested more in the traditional light industries such as textiles, food stuffs and other manufactures. These three categories have accounted for well over half of Japan's investment in manufacturing. The United States, on the other hand, has invested more in the technologically advanced fields of electrical machinery, transportation equipment and chemicals. Although detailed information on all the Asian countries is not available to bring out these differences, a few countries have published the necessary information.

Modes of Operation

What are the major distinctions in modes of operations of the Japanese and American firms? We can distinguish a few areas in which the firms of the two nations differ, and these will be explored below.

In Thailand, 43 percent of Japanese investment is in textiles and apparel, as contrasted with 3 percent for the United States. In Indonesia, of a total Japanese manufacturing investment of $45 million, textiles and light industry account for over 75 percent, whereas chemicals and heavy industry represent over 50 percent of United States investment in manufacturing. In South Korea, Japan accounts for over 60 percent of all foreign investment in textiles and apparel, whereas the United States accounts for over 70 percent of all foreign investment in transportation equipment and over 67 percent in electrical machinery and equipment.

Admittedly, the data are very spotty on which to make such a generalization but the Economic Commission for Asia and the Far East did conclude in reference to developing Asia:

> . . . United States investments [tend] to be large and to be concentrated in oil or mineral development, or technologically advanced fields such as electric/electronic manufacturing and chemicals . . . Japanese investments tend to be smaller and to be directed to lighter industries. . .[4]

Table 12–1 presents the official direct investment statistics of both Japan and the U.S. for individual Asian countries on an accumulated basis through 1971.

Ownership. Typically, the Japanese have been more willing to allow local equity participation in their ventures in Asia than have the Americans. A number of explanations have been offered to account for this distinction. One is that the Japanese seem to be more able to deal with minority interests than do the United States firms. Another is that the Japanese government has pushed some firms into joint ventures to lower the profile of the Japanese companies in Southeast Asia. Another is that host Asian countries have been more insistent that local equity is involved in Japanese projects than they have been for American firms. Korea, for example, did not allow Japanese companies to establish wholly owned subsidiaries until recently. Then there is also the fact

Table 12–1.   Accumulated U.S. and Japanese Direct Investment in Developing Asia—1971 *(millions of dollars)*[5]

	U.S.	*Japan*	*Total*
Ceylon	*	2	
Taiwan	133	85	218
Hong Kong	286	139	427
India	329	12	341
Indonesia	512	241	753
So. Korea	277	33	310
Malaysia, Singapore	307	50, 33	390
Pakistan	96	5	101
Philippines	719	74	793
Thailand	124	91	215
Other	266	5	271
	3,049	770	3,819

that the Japanese restrictions on capital outflow from Japan have necessitated utilizing local capital in a number of overseas projects.

Finally, there is the question of the technological level of the investment. The United States often invests abroad to exploit a particular technique or process. Local participation in management may be seen as incompatible with the need for secrecy. Most of Japan's investment has been in raw materials or in standard manufacturing lines. Here there would seem to be less objection to allowing local participation in management. However, as Japan moves up the line to more sophisticated manufacturing processes, it too may resist local participation more than in the past.

Joint ventures are frequently more symbolic than real. One student of Japanese investment in Asia has noted a tendency of the Japanese firms to select as a local partner a national who has had no previous experience in the particular industry. This suggests that the Japanese are looking for a silent partner in the business and don't mind creating a few "instant millionaires" in the process.

Some observers have noted an increased willingness on the part of U.S. corporations abroad to "live with" local equity. It is seen as being an asset in recruiting local talent as well as a method to "grease the way" through the bureaucracy. As United States firms are forced to compete with a growing Japanese presence, there will be added incentive to allow as much local participation as possible.

Rationale. Apart from a heavy investment in petroleum exploration and related activities, the major thrust of United States investment into Asia in recent years seems to have been motivated by the growth in foreign sourcing or component manufacture and assembly. Much of the United States direct investment in Hong Kong, Singapore, Taiwan and South Korea is of this type. Although the small export-oriented economies of Asia have accounted for most of the United States foreign sourcing, some is also recorded in Thailand, the Philippines and Indonesia.

In the case of Japan, raw material acquisition has played a more important role in their Asian investment. Japan, which must import nearly 80 percent of all its raw materials, has had to continually seek out new sources of supply. In 1968, over $170 million in foreign investments went into natural resources development. In 1969, it was over $314 million, and accounted for half of all foreign investment in that year. During 1951–1969, approximately 45 percent of the total Japanese direct investment in Asia was in the extractive industries.

Japanese manufacturing investment has been both of the import substitution variety and of the export-oriented or sourcing variety. Of the latter, it has gone largely to Taiwan, South Korea and Hong Kong. In fact, Japan's growing stake in South Korea and Taiwan has prompted some observers to comment that the two countries are becoming merely extensions of the Japanese economy.

There are a number of examples of this. Japan applies duty on the value added only of goods sent to Korea for assembly. Rather than encourage labor immigration, the Japanese companies are going to the labor, and the labor closest to home. Japan is also considering placing some of its oil refining and metal processing establishments in Korea to reduce pollution of the already highly polluted environment. This "exporting of pollution" is likely to continue.

To what degree this movement into South Korea and Taiwan will be slowed by Chou En-lai's enunciation of the "Four Principles" of Sino–Japanese trade in the spring of 1970 is difficult to predict.[6] Some people argue that the Japanese government-business cooperation is so effective that certain companies will be selected to remain "untainted" so as to be able to take advantage of future Chinese–Japanese trade opportunities. Recent reports from both South Korea and Taiwan suggest that the slowing in Japanese investment activity which took place in the last six months of 1971 and through most of 1972 has been reversed.

Government-Business Relations. It is often said that the degree of cooperation or collusion between the Japanese firms and the Japanese government is a close, harmonious working relationship. This relationship, which is sometimes called "Japan, Incorporated" by foreigners, is usually contrasted with the relationship between government and business in the United States. On close examination, however, it is difficult to document any qualitative difference in treatment: both countries have risk insurance programs available, assist in financing projects, and supply private firms with economic intelligence concerning markets, laws, customs and likely difficulties.

Japanese-American Cooperation

In some fields, Japan and the United States have invested in Asia on a joint basis. Some mineral investment projects have been multilateral private ventures as distinguished from joint ventures. Here a multilateral venture refers to three or more participants of different nationalities. Multinational ventures among Japanese, United States and local interests have taken place in mineral development, banking and in oil exploration. Originally, many of these multinational or consortium arrangements involved United States participation in the financing of the project because of Japanese balance of payments constraints. But, increasingly, consortium arrangements involve joint management as well. And with the growing concern over the national identity of foreign investment in both host and source countries, this trend is likely to continue. The attractiveness of this form of investment cooperation increases when one considers the sensitivity to foreign business pressure likely to exist during the reconstruction phase of the Indochina settlement.

HOST COUNTRY ATTITUDES

General Receptivity

For the Asian region as a whole it is generally accepted that the receptivity toward foreign investment is considerably improved over a decade ago when most foreign investment was branded as a form of neocolonialism. This is partly a result of the example of success; those countries which have grown the fastest (Taiwan, South Korea, Hong Kong and Singapore) have deliberately encourated the inflow of foreign investment. But probably the most important reason has been the absence of a single dominating industrial country investing in the region. This is in sharp contrast to the case of Latin America. Substantial investment positions in Asia are maintained by Great Britain, the United States and Japan. Recognizable investment presences are maintained by France, the Netherlands, Germany and Switzerland. Very importantly, a considerable amount of inter-Asian investment has occurred. Hong Kong, Taiwan and Singapore investors have gone into Malaysia, Thailand, Indonesia and the Philippines. This diversity of investment sources has had much to do with the concept of foreign investment not being viewed as strictly a neo-colonialist ploy to infringe on the sovereignty of the host country.

The experience of Asia as host for foreign investment suggests that the principle of "countervailing power" is of major importance. In overly simplistic terms, it can be stated that foreign investment dominance by one country is destabilizing and is likely to lead to growing frustration and hostility, but if the foreign investment position is distributed among a number of countries (more being better than few), it is seen as less of a threat and more of a benefit to the development process. Or, as the former Indonesian ambassador to the United States has put it:

> It is in our national interest to involve as many countries as possible in the economic development of Indonesia. In this light, neutrality is removed from the impact of economic pressures because these tend to cancel each other out.[7]

Direct investment as distinct from economic aid or portfolio investment is seen to offer a variety of benefits to the developing countries. First, there are the more traditional benefits, including contributing to the foreign exchange holdings of the receiving country, stimulating domestic savings and investment, and providing employment opportunities and markets for suppliers. To these benefits have to be added others which, to the present day development planners, have potentially greater importance for development. These include access to technology; the establishment of contacts with overseas banks, capital markets, and factor and product markets; the training of workers and creation of indigenous skills in administrative, financial, marketing and other business techniques; and the development of a class of skilled local managers and entrepreneurs. With respect to manufacturing projects, they frequently have greater employment impact (especially in urban areas), have more "spill-over" effects upon the local economy—skills transferred to other "new" sectors, and demand for local fabricating and material supply—and open up to the country new technologies unobtainable by other means.

Given this list of perceived benefits it is little wonder that the kind of overseas firm most coveted by the developing countries of Asia is not the extractive firm, nor the manufacturing firm assembling or producing solely for the local market, but the multinational firm whose local production facilities are integrated into a global production and marketing system.

In general, then, private foreign investment is perceived by most Asian developing countries as playing an important role in the modernization process implied by development. This is less true of investment in nonmanufacturing activities, but even here its contribution is recognized. Yet few if any Asians see this investment as costless. In country after country attempts are being made, via legislative action and other means, to maximize the associated benefits and minimize the costs.

Any enumeration of the costs associated with foreign investment normally includes noneconomic as well as economic considerations. Below we attempt to sort out these issues and identify the most often heard complaints. The costs are listed under the headings: economic, sovereignty and culture.

Economic

The economic costs of foreign investment are usually described as potential or future costs. They tend to center on how the policies of the foreign corporation may stunt the development of indigenous techniques and skills. For example, although the access to the research and development performed by the parent company is an acknowledged benefit of foreign investment, the complaint is frequently voiced that this access may be bought at the cost of a reduced national R&D capacity. The same fear is voiced over the development of domestic managerial and entrepreneurial skills. Importing such skills in the form of foreign subsidiaries or joint ventures may reduce incentives for host country development.

With respect to capital flow, it is agreed that capital inflow adds to aggregate savings and investment, but there is concern that the development of a domestic capital market may be inhibited. This concern is increased when the question of foreign banking interests is raised. As is well known, the large multinational corporations like doing business with their traditional banks, and during the postwar period when the multinationals have invested abroad, so have their banks. This is most true for Europe, but it is also happening in the rest of the world. Dominance by foreign banking interests is a real fear in most Asian nations, and therefore, restrictions on such activity are the rule in many countries.

Another fear has to do with the sort of technology utilized by the foreign firm. The complaint is frequently heard that too often the technology used is more appropriate to the factor endowment of the source country than that of the host country. Production processes are said to be more capital intensive than is warranted, given the labor surpluses in most Asian nations. However, Helen Hughes argues, based on her study of foreign investment in Southeast Asia, that there is little hard evidence supporting this view and that where such evidence exists it is often the result of excessively protectionistic policies adopted by the host countries themselves, which subsidizes capital-intensive techniques.[8]

A final economic cost has to do with the ability of multinational corporations to reduce its subsidiary's tax liability to the host country by arbitrary transfer pricing or adjustments of service fees and the allocation of administrative costs. By pricing components supplied to the subsidiary at excessive levels, the income subject to tax in the host country can be reduced. Capable tax administrators can sometimes prevent this, but in developing countries they are in limited supply.

Sovereignty

A second category of arguments raised against foreign investment has to do with the threat it poses to a country's independence or sovereignty. More intangible than the economic costs enumerated above, this concern is nonetheless frequently given the greatest weight in the developing countries. Such arguments range from the belief that the presence of foreign subsidiaries interferes with developmental planning in the host country, to the belief that the subsidiary is an operating extention of the foreign policy of the source country's government. Kindleberger in referring to the perceived political costs of foreign investment stresses:

> ... the uneasiness that many people instinctively have when they contemplate the fact that the activities of institutions within their economy and polity are "controlled" from outside the political unit.[9]

And when the perceived threat of foreign control issues from one of the world's superpowers, such concerns are multiplied.

Although there do not seem to be many documented examples to support this thesis, enough exist to cause discomfort to host countries. The United States has extended its antitrust policies to subsidiaries of United States parent firms abroad. It has prohibited exports from subsidiaries to certain communist nations and has influenced dividend policies of subsidiaries through its investment control program.

Little more can be said on this issue except that the fear does exist, and probably will continue to color the relations between the host and source country throughout the seventies. It should be added that the perceived threat of foreign control is intensified by ownership policies biased against joint ventures and local participation.

Cultural

A final category of costs of foreign investment refers to the clash between the cultures of the host and source countries. Most Asians have grown up with the concept of the "Ugly American." What is new to the Asian situation in the seventies is the recognition that Americans have no monopoly on "ugliness." Increasingly, the Japanese are coming in for the same sorts of criticisms initially directed at the Americans.

The Japanese businessman is accused of being excessively aggressive, arrogant and clannish. He is accused of discrimination in his employment practices and of being unconcerned with the development of the local economy. He is supposedly insensitive to local traditions and customs, and is resented for his sexual appetite away from home. These complaints are subsumed under the titles: "Ugly Japanese," "Yellow Yankee" and "Economic Animal."

Perhaps resentment of this sort tends to focus on the most recent source of irritation. Americans may not behave differently, but in Asia today they seem to be less criticized for their cultural offenses. One must not fail to consider the possibility that a learning process is at work and that businessmen and officials can learn or be induced to adapt.

INDUCEMENTS AND RESTRICTIONS

The developing countries of Asia have almost all instituted specific inducements to encourage the inflow of foreign investment. Yet there has been little uniformity in policies and the degree of inducement varies widely from country to country.

At the administrative level, a positive measure to encourage foreign investment has been the centralization of the decision-making machinery in an office of foreign investment or a foreign investment board. Most of the countries have such an office and its existence has tended to reduce administrative delay and costly exploration.

At another level, most Asian countries have adopted a set of investment priorities. Although all industrial areas are usually open to foreign investment (apart from banking), a preferred list of industries typically exists, and investment in such industries makes a firm eligible for a wide range of investment incentives. These are called "pioneer" industries in Malaysia and Singapore, "preferred" industries in the Philippines and "promotable" industries in Thailand. Such preferred industries are typically those showing import replacement or export promotion potential, and increasingly those with the maximum potential linkages to the rest of the economy.

Incentives offered by the host country governments for investment in the invited industries primarily apply to taxation status, but other incentives are offered as well. Tax incentives include reduced corporate tax rates, tax holidays ranging from up to ten years for all or part of a company's profits, accelerated depreciation, personal income tax exemptions for foreign personel and carry-forward of losses. Other incentives used include investment subsidies, concession on import duties paid on inputs, foreign exchange allowances, credit subsidies and low cost infrastructure facilities (e.g. cheap power or free land).

Practice in the use of these incentives has enabled the officials in the developing countries to become fairly sophisticated in discriminating in favor of firms advancing priority development goals. For example, tax holidays have been lengthened for firms investing in specific regions of a developing country and thus reducing congestion in the port cities. Firms meeting certain export goals have benefited through reduced tax rates or longer holidays, and in Malaysia firms can increase their tax holiday by using a specific proportion of domestic materials as inputs. This "fine tuning" is likely to increase in the future and specific incentives will increasingly be linked to exports, to labor policies (including the upgrading of skills), and to growth in domestic value-added and ownership policies.

It is not in the interests of any Asian state to trigger a competitive "war" in the bidding to attract investment. Each incentive offered has a real economic cost associated with it, and care must be taken to avoid diverting all the "economic rent" to the foreign company. To head off such a development, nations of Asia (perhaps through ASEAN and ECAFE) should agree on a host country investment code which would limit the list of allowable incentives.

Obviously, the strength of each country's bargaining position with the foreign firm varies greatly. Labor-short Singapore for example can afford to be much more selective than can, say, Indonesia. But the direction of the movement is clear, and the typical package of benefits and costs brought by the foreign firm will be required to be increasingly weighted toward the developing country's advantage.

The question of ownership must be seen in this light. Wholly owned foreign firms will continue to be allowed entry into most of the developing Asian nations, but on a very selective basis. The cost to the host country will only be tolerated in those cases where the benefits associated with foreign entry are seen as vital to the development process. This will be true for only few firms. Put another way, a foreign firm will find that it will have to offer fewer benefits to the host country if it will tolerate local equity participation.

THE FUTURE

Foreign investment in Asia promises continued expansion throughout the decade of the seventies. There are a number of lines of reasoning supporting this prediction. First, the Asian developing countries will continue to maintain a qualified "open door" policy regarding overseas investment. These nations, however, can be expected to increase the stringency of the tests that each new project must meet. Moreover, the origin and identity of investment projects will become increasingly important considerations in the deliberations of the various investment boards throughout the region.

More important to the prediction of continued investment growth in the region are the conditions in both Japan and the United States, the chief investors in the area. In both countries, the economic forces spurring investment in the region will intensify. Japan, faced with a developing labor shortage, a growing concern for the environment and increased protectionism in its leading markets, will accelerate its outflow of capital rapidly. The recent loosening of investment controls and the upward revaluation of the yen will also contribute to the growth in foreign investment.

United States investment in Asia will also accelerate over the next decade, as the trends for the last several years already indicate. Most investment models point to greater United States investment in Asia, and the recent dollar devaluation will not materially affect this trend.

Within Asia, and increasingly throughout the world, the United States will see in Japan its chief economic competitor. As the large Japanese corporations, led by the giant trading companies, move out into the world for production purposes as well as trade, they will trigger defensive investment reactions by United States corporations. A recent listing by *Fortune* of the 300 largest industrial companies outside of the United States, show that Japan headed the list with 79 companies, Britain having fallen to second place with 61, followed by Germany and France with 43 and 31 respectively.[10] These large Japanese corporations, having acquired the knowledge of operating abroad, an awareness of world market conditions and, most importantly, the financial and technical resources to facilitate foreign investment, are poised for major expansion in their overseas investment. This will be the most important new dimension in foreign investment during the seventies and promises to make Asia the scene of the most intense investment activity since the European wave of the late fifties and early sixties.

It is true that there is growing opposition within the United States to allowing United States corporations to invest freely abroad. Of major concern to the American labor movement is the job loss associated with the migration of production facilities. This concern has most recently been manifested in labor's support of the Hartke-Burke trade and investment bill now before Congress, which includes provisions for limiting investment out-flows. The defeat of this bill, the course of action urged by most economists, should not be interpreted as a clean bill of health for overseas investment. With any major form of international economic interaction, problems will emerge. What must be sought is the proper machinery, both national and international, to address the problems and to seek solutions in a mutually beneficial manner.

Foreign investment will continue as a major force in the world economy, and it is naive to assume that absence of any control measures would maximize benefits either to host and source countries, or to the investing company. We have mentioned the operation of investment boards in host countries. Yet, control at the source is also warranted. Both Japan and the United States should create some type of investment institution which would operate to coordinate existing flows of investment, and facilitate the resolution of existing disputes so as to allow the continuance of mutually beneficial private flows of capital throughout Asia.

NOTES TO CHAPTER TWELVE

1. Direct investment involves actual control of the enterprises through ownership of a sufficient percentage of the firms' total equity. This contrasts with portfolio investment which does not involve control but merely the right to a percentage of the earnings. This paper will be concerned only with direct investment, since it is by far the most important type of private capital going to the developing countries of Asia.

2. British investment in Asia, although large, will not be treated in this paper. It tends to be concentrated in India, Pakistan, Ceylon and Malaysia, was largely of the colonial variety, is growing slowly and will soon be exceeded by Japanese investment. Britain's entry into the Common Market may further reduce its interests in the region.

3. Data on United States direct investment printed in this section were obtained from the United States Department of Commerce, *Survey of Current Business* (various issues), Washington, D.C.

4. *Economic Survey of Asia and the Far East 1970, Part I: The Role of Foreign Private Investment in Economic Development and Cooperation in the ECAFE* (Bangkok, 1971), p. 109.

5. Japanese data were obtained from MITI, *Economic Cooperation–Present Status and Problems, 1970.* These data are on an approved basis and exclude reinvested earnings but include long-term private loans. United States data were obtained from the *Survey of Current Business,* October 1970, and reinvested earnings, and are computed on a current year transaction basis. (Some individual country figures were provided in unpublished form by the Office of Business Economics, Department of Commerce.)

6. The "Four Principles" are that no Japanese firm can expect trade with China which has:
    1. assisted the aggressive regimes on Taiwan and in South Korea,
    2. invested in either Taiwan or South Korea,

3. supplied munitions to the United States for use in the Indochina War, or

4. had joint ventures with United States firms.

Pacific Basin Reports, May 15, 1971.

7. Soedjatmoko, *Asia* (Autumn 1970): p. 21. The ambassador also has pointed out that the diffusion of foreign investment positions is a positive force in reducing "major power antagonisms" in the region and in supporting the "low involvement posture of the external powers in the military and political fields," in "The Role of the Major Powers in the East Asian–Pacific Region" (Speech given at a conference on Prospects for Peace, Development and Security in Asia in the 1970s, May 20–23, 1971, Airlie House, Warrenton, Virginia).

8. H. Hughes, "An Assessment of Policies Towards Foreign Investment in the Asian–Pacific Region" (Paper given at the Third Pacific Trade and Development Conference, Sydney, Australia, August 1970), p. 26.

9. C. P. Kindleberger, *American Investment Abroad* (New Haven: Yale University Press, 1969), p. 5.

10. See *Fortune* September 1973, p. 203.

Chapter Thirteen

Comments

Carl Jayarajah

There is a considerable body of evidence to show that trade inter-dependence among countries in the Pacific Basin has increased in recent years. The establishment of a free trade area embracing Australia, Canada, Japan, New Zealand and the United States is likely to intensify this interdependence. In particular, Japanese exports to Australia, Canada, New Zealand and the United States will expand, while exports of agricultural products of other members are likely to find bigger markets in Japan, in addition of course to competitive industrial products.

The creation of a free trade area of this size is, however, likely to have an impact on the rest of the world, both among the developed and less developed countries. In the absence of a liberal trading arrangement and special measures, nonmembers would find market penetration in PAFTA more difficult. It may even exacerbate problems associated with an economic detente between the U.S. and the EEC. Further, if the less developed primary producer countries are adversely affected, they may be induced to work out separate arrangements with other trading blocs, compartmentalizing international trade. Finally, one should not overestimate Japan's ability to open her markets; the official view has consistently been that a policy of caution is clearly indicated with regard to the utilization of foreign exchange reserves. In view of the evolving Japanese diplomatic initiatives vis-à-vis the U.S.S.R. and China, the ability and willingness of Japan to participate in schemes of this nature still remains a matter for conjecture.

If trade expansion is the primary objective, one is hopeful that recent steps toward establishing an orderly international monetary system and forthcoming initiatives toward the dismantling of tariff and nontariff barriers on a nondiscriminatory basis, combined with the application of speedy and effective balance of payments adjustment mechanisms, will make equally effective contributions to the goal of an economically strong, prosperous and peaceful Pacific Basin.

129

Foreign private investment has and will continue to play an important role in facilitating the economic progress of less developed countries. In recent years, however, certain issues which divide investors and host governments have gained strength. In the case of "mature investments," such as plantations, host governments feel that capital has been repatriated many times over; indigenous control of the investment is then sought. Those investments in the category of "commanding heights"—power, telecommunications and other public utilities, or those industries accounting for a significant proportion of national output—are supposed to be of strategic economic and political importance. Governments of developing countries also wish to exercise control over industries having balance of payments implications—whether in terms of their demand for raw materials and maintenance imports, or for repatriation of dividends and capital—particularly when high demand and inflationary conditions persist at home. The degree, manner and appropriateness of the technology transferred by foreign private investment is another bone of contention. Finally, there is the clash of interest with domestic elites—indigenous businessmen and the bureaucracy. With the former, competition may center on products, as well as access to resources—financial, manpower and raw material. The bureaucracy may be affected by a disruption of the structure of wages and salaries and the oft evident tendency of foreign private investors to deal directly with politicians.

The success of foreign private investors depends upon their ability to harmonize their activity with the interests of three specific groups: politicians, the bureaucracy and trade unions. The avoidance of open confrontations with governments and the provision of tangible evidence of contribution to the economy and the balance of payments of host countries is of fundamental significance. The willingness to sell out the interest in due time and to move into other industries or to diversify equity structures needs to be combined with an avoidance of market exploitation and the aggrandizement of available local finance. The close tie-up of trade unions and politicians is another factor to be reckoned with; hence the development of harmonious relationships will result in considerable real dividends to the foreign private investor. To this end, the selection of the right managers and staff for overseas posting is a paramount requisite; all too often head office rejects are given sinecures abroad at considerable risk to the expatriate investment.

Part IV

**Strategies for the Pacific
in the 1970s and 1980s**

Chapter Fourteen

Introduction

Bernard K. Gordon

Since 1968, beginning with the abdication of Lyndon Johnson and the election of Richard Nixon, there has been a standstill on issues and questions of Pacific strategy. Before then, indeed throughout the postwar era, the United States had been the one firm mooring in issues of Pacific region security. Many nations had based their military planning assumptions, and much of their strategic doctrine, on this one paramount feature of the Pacific environment. But change was signaled in the events of 1968; it was then underlined when President Nixon and Dr. Kissinger spoke at Guam in 1969 (thereby announcing the "Nixon Doctrine"); and it was made undeniably clear after mid–1971 with the White House visits to China and the seemingly harsher American tone toward Japan. The consequence for many nations was to call into question the strategic assumptions of a whole generation, and to demand that they be re-examined.

Yet despite the changes indicated by the U.S. since 1968 (and certainly not later than 1971), it is also clear in 1973–74 that no coherent set of principles or assumptions has emerged—from any quarter—which resembles a new Pacific region security framework. We have instead only the beginnings of some understandings of the elements that *might* eventually substitute somewhat for the previous *Pax Americana,* and we have a very large number of questions that will need to be answered before any patterns of a new order in the Pacific become clear. We do not know, for example, what role to expect of Australia—a state which has long depended upon British and American guarantees for ultimate security, but which was consequently prepared to act energetically and forthrightly, far from its borders. We know that Australians are unsatisfied with the present seeming absence of a foreign policy for their country, but we do not know, for example, how widespread is the view that argues for a nuclear-armed, and somewhat isolationist, "fortress Australia."

We know even less of China's likely role during the next decade[1] —for only now are we beginning to achieve some clarity with regard to the foreign and military policies adopted by China in the past decade. Many observers of China are convinced that China has had only slight and sporadic involvement in events beyond its borders, but it is not yet certain how much of China's behavior during the 1960s was merely the outward manifestation of intense turmoil within and how much was the consequence of a clear and coherent program. As the evidence now stands, there is much persuasiveness to the view that China had little more than a reactive East Asian policy during the 1960s, and made its presence and views known largely when it was impossible to remain silent and altogether uninvolved. It is not certain whether this pattern of Chinese underinvolvement will continue, or whether—if that *is* what existed—a more self-confident and prosperous China, in a period of détente with the Americans, will now feel itself free to act with more energy and impact in East Asian affairs.

Most uncertain, potentially most worrisome, and most talked about, of course, is what sometimes seems to be the formless unknown of Japan's foreign and defense policies. All observers are almost literally in the dark with reference to Japan's interests and policies during the next period, and there is almost as much confusion and puzzlement about both the substance and the process of Japanese foreign policy during the past ten years as well. Among the many questions for which there are no satisfactory answers are the preferences of Japanese leaders regarding the future of the U.S.–Japan Security Treaty; the likelihood that Japan might undertake some form of direct involvement in security problems of the Asia–Pacific region beyond the home islands; the prospects for major and intensive Japanese cooperation with the U.S.S.R. for the development of Siberian resources; and the extent to which the so-called "Nixon shocks" of 1971 really led to a significant rethinking of Japan's overall security and foreign policy posture.

What these questions point to (and the list easily could be extended) is that we appear to be at the end of an era in Pacific region international politics, with few guidelines about the future and with many ingredients that would contribute toward shaping policy quite hidden from view. At the same time, it has to be recognized that East Asia and the Pacific continues to represent a very high potential for turmoil and conflict,[2] and the need for achieving at least great-power stability in the region is of pressing urgency. Finally, it is probably useful to recall that the Pacific rim of Asia has experienced more profound political transformations in the years since World War II than any other major global region.

The major factor that sets East Asia aside is that the widely used concept of "multipolarity" appears to have reasonable application today only in this region. For it is only on the Pacific Asian rim that each of the world's most powerful and prominent states—the U.S., China, the U.S.S.R. and Japan—identifies some or all of its vital national interests. From an American perspective it is also important to recognize that this characteristic of multipolarity in

East Asia has been a goal sought and nurtured by United States foreign policy behavior throughout at least the past generation.

Both these factors need constantly to be kept in mind, especially by Americans, for they represent both a new environment for United States policy and a challenge in the sense that the accomplishment of any goal calls for a review of the policies that led to its achievement. In the early years of this century, for example, the United States sought to be one of the several interacting powers on the Pacific rim. That was an era, brought to mind by the "open door" label, in which it would have been factually accurate to speak of "multipolarity" since Britain, Germany, France, Japan and Russia were all involved, in large part to prevent any one of the others from achieving a position of dominance, especially over the weakened Chinese "empire." But it was a short-lived international structure, for the onset of World War I caused the withdrawal of the European powers from region and they never effectively returned. Indeed, much of American foreign policy toward the region during the 1920s and 1930s, as I have noted elsewhere, was shaped as if the multipolar balance still existed.[3]

Thus we sought to encourage the British, the Dutch, the French (and anyone else who would listen), to adopt a firmer stance to the increasingly expansionist policies and behavior of the Japanese, beginning as early as their "Twenty-One Demands" against China in 1915. Beginning with the Manchurian aggression in 1931, however, and undeniably after 1937, it was clear that none of the previously involved states were interested in or capable of effective opposition to the direction and thrust of Japanese policies. It was from that period that we have to date the beginning of bipolarity in the Pacific Asian region. For after Franklin Roosevelt's essentially ignored "quarantine" speech, in which he asked that other states join in measures to isolate and thwart Japan's policies of expansion, American leaders reluctantly began to conclude that no other state would act in concert with the United States for that purpose.

What then ensued, of course, was a thirty year period of American unilateral behavior in the Pacific region. This was aimed first at Japan, and, in the post–World War II period, at the containment of "communist" efforts forcefully to bring about political change in the region of East and Southeast Asia. Of course the United States erred in believing for a period that China and the Soviet Union acted as a "bloc" for this purpose, but this does not detract from the point that the United States acted singlemindedly and singlehandedly in the postwar era to resist and frustrate efforts to overthrow governments or to bring about change through war and externally aided revolution.

I say a "thirty year period" because the announcement of the Nixon Doctrine in 1969 formally signaled that the U.S. would no longer be willing to act alone to accomplish these goals. It is in that respect that observers accurately and generally reported that after the Nixon Doctrine the United States' view of the Asia Pacific region was one of strategic multipolarity. But what is less readily evident is that the Nixon Doctrine simply formalized, in unmistakeable terms, the actual trend of American policy in the Pacific since shortly after the end of World War II: to recreate something like the pre–1914 balance of power (or multipolarity) that had briefly characterized the region in the years when the United States entered the Pacific scene.

It was this goal which led the U.S. to reverse, as early as 1948, its initially harsh occupation of Japan, in order to help rebuild that nation to the point where Tokyo would once again play a role of major importance in Pacific affairs. It was a similar concern with "multipolarity" that led the U.S., despite the victory of the Chinese Communists in 1949, to avoid a full break with Peking until months after the outbreak of the Korean war.[4] Even in the late Eisenhower years, as memories of direct Chinese involvement in that war waned, the U.S. reopened its dialogue with China, and shortly before the death of President Kennedy, his administration went very far toward extending an olive branch to Peking. The instrument was an important San Francisco speech of the assistant secretary of state for East Asia Pacific affairs (Hilsman), early in 1963. But as had been the case with the Korean War, whatever hopes existed for a resumed communication with China were then interrupted by the reality of the war in Vietnam, and were put aside for the duration of the 1960s.

The other side of this same coin, of course, was that the U.S. was intensively engated, in the twenty years between 1950–70, in military, political and economic "shoring up" efforts at many points on the Asia Pacific rim. The events to recall are the military response in Korea itself; the SEATO Treaty in 1954; the even earlier mutual security treaties with Australia, New Zealand and the Philippines; the multiplicity of aid efforts throughout the region; and finally, from 1962–63 on, the enormous energies devoted somehow to preventing the incorporation of South Vietnam by Hanoi. All of these were part of an effort to convince indigenous as well as external leaders that an East Asia not dominated by any one state or scheme of things could be achieved. In very large part, that realization has now been accomplished. The overall environment of greater security and political stability, as well as economic improvement, is far more optimistic than most observers would have predicted in 1950.

But that is precisely the dilemma for the United States during the next period—the decade 1975–85. Through great effort and cost, American policies have met with considerable success in the Pacific region—at least insofar as the overall international structure of the region is concerned. For even in the face of continuing problems (Laos and Cambodia, for example) and disappointments (the Philippines and Burma), there are positive developments that reflect this structure. Among these is the fact that we now find in Southeast Asia a group of politically cooperating and economically improving states (Indonesia, Malaysia, Thailand, Singapore); a strong, prosperous and politically stable Japan that is able and increasingly willing to contribute to constructive change throughout the pacific; and, finally, a China that is quite obviously not dependent upon the U.S.S.R. and appears willing to moderate its international behavior.[5] These are goals long aimed for by the United States, and the question that now has to be faced is how we and others will relate to this changed and considerably improved environment. The habits of a generation reflect an American role (as Senator Fulbright has said about our worldwide posture) as the solitary "policeman" of the Pacific, and we have had no reason up to now to develop policies and attitudes appropriate to a multipolar Asia. Now that multipolarity increasingly does seem to describe the structure of politics on the Asia Pacific rim, it is important to ask whether we know what to do with it.

One approach—which will be very difficult to resist—will be to call for a posture of accelerated disengagement from our past very heavy involvement in the region. Some observers, of course, already recommend an American Pacific policy tantamount to withdrawal. That is very unlikely to come about, but it is also necessary to recognize that the deep Sino–Soviet split, and the impressive capabilities of Japan, will lead many sensible Americans to argue that "we have done enough," and that the competitive presence of these several powerful nations allows us safely to withdraw back to Hawaii. However appealing that notion is on first examination, it needs to be resisted.

The major reason is that a posture of significant American disengagement, especially one that implies ultimate withdrawal, is altogether likely to cause such states as Australia and Japan to consider radical transformations in their security policies. Japan, for example, is suspicious both of China and the Soviet Union, and would not wish either of those two states to achieve too powerful a position in East Asia. Yet Japan has little confidence in its own ability to prevent that outcome—in the event, for example, that the present enmity between Peking and Moscow worsens and leads even to Sino–Soviet hostilities. Moreover, many Japanese are opposed in any event to the adoption of policies designed to achieve a more independent Japanese security role—even if there were greater confidence in the nation's capabilities. In this respect the U.S.–Japan alliance is a central and essential element of Japan's foreign policy, for it enables Tokyo to avoid and escape the need to consider any unilateral alternatives.

But should confidence in the American presence significantly decline, then Japan increasingly would be led to consider profoundly different approaches. One of these is the prospect of achieving some form of alignment or close relationship with either the U.S.S.R. or China. Such a development—to the extent that it meant a linking-up of Japan's enormous economic capabilities to the political and military perspectives of either the U.S.S.R. or China—would of course represent an awesome prospect for the United States. Indeed, it would signal the ultimate denial of those Pacific region goals toward which U.S. foreign policy has aimed for much of this century.

An initially more likely choice for Japan, in the event that confidence in its American connection were significantly eroded, arises in the more familiar context of a Japanese decision either to "go nuclear," or otherwise to adopt a much more independent security policy. This, too, has few attractions, either from the perspective of the U.S. or in the broader framework of Pacific region security, for it is quite likely that Japanese policies that sooner or later implied nuclear armaments would also trigger widespread proliferation elsewhere, and would certainly lead to stern and destabilizing reactions from both China and the Soviet Union. Any one of these potential developments is less desirable than the present situation, however unsettled today's Asia may appear to be.

Similar considerations, though on a reduced scale, apply to such states as Australia (which has a readily achievable nuclear potential), and Indonesia. For both of these governments the prospect of a continued "forward" presence of the U.S. in the Pacific is a security crutch—often decried in public rhetoric while quietly endorsed and accepted in fact. The Australian dilemma is the more immediate, since there are already voices calling for an independent nuclear capability, and others which have argued that the traditional reliance on the U.S. is worth no more today than was the earlier one on Britain—until that was found wanting in 1941—42. Indeed, some Australians (including a cabinet minister who shortly thereafter lost his post) have called for a new relationship with the U.S.S.R., presumably to help "balance" China's resurgence in the Pacific.

This is not the place to examine each of these national perspectives in any detail. What does need to be emphasized, however, is that the U.S. has given little evidence so far of an ability either to reassure former dependent states or to benefit creatively from the "independence" urgings which the Nixon Doctrine helped set in motion. Instead, American policy toward almost all Asia Pacific states other than China has appeared to be characterized by a business-as-usual stance, even while its own relations with both China and the U.S.S.R. are evidently undergoing major change. Of course, it is in relation to Japan that this inconsistency is most clear, and the Japanese (as will be seen from other contributions in this book) are altogether aware of the problem. What the following chapters also suggest is that American policies toward Japan, which were sufficient through most of the postwar era (and which were largely of a patron-client character), are in need of much more sophistication.

The term that comes to mind, increasingly suggested by observers, is for a greater degree of "partnership" in the U.S.–Japan relationship. Understandably, this quality has been lacking in all aspects of U.S. relations with every other Pacific region state, for the simple reason that no other state was capable of playing roles of equality with the U.S. In many respects, measured in military capability and economic and industrial prominence, that imbalance will continue for many years. But to the extent that the U.S. is now intent upon some degree of Pacific disengagement, the relative gap between the U.S. and several other Asian Pacific states will narrow, and the implication for the United States is a policy far less characterized than in the past by unilateral initiatives.

Although a posture of more genuine "partnership" in the Pacific will represent many problems of adjustment for the U.S., it also holds out many attractions, particularly if we mean what we have said by hoping to shift the postwar security burden partly to other shoulders. The negotiating task itself will be extremely difficult, for the concept calls for a balance in which the U.S. will hope to encourage other states to "do more," while at the same time reassuring those states that the U.S. does not mean thereby to leave them out on the proverbial limb, alone.

Fortunately, there are leaders in the region whose approach to this problem is both imaginative and sophisticated, and who want to find ways to cooperate with the United States in achieving this balance. Those who come most prominently to mind are in Thailand, Japan, Indonesia and Singapore. Prime Minister Lee Kwan Yew of Singapore, for example, already has proposed one far-reaching format which deserves to be considered very seriously. He has called for a naval security format under which Australia, Japan, the United States and several interested Southeast Asian nations would together develop a joint naval capacity for Pacific and Southeast Asian waters.[6] In part his proposal seems designed to counter the prospect of an increased Soviet naval role in the Pacific, for as Lee personally is aware, the Soviets already have asked that various states provide "calling in" facilities for Soviet naval ships. Singapore has had a difficult time turning away these Soviet requests, and it is widely suspected that India and perhaps others already have cooperated with Moscow for the construction of baselike facilities at several points on the Indian Ocean littoral.

At the same time, and as observers of Japan know, there is much concern in Tokyo with continued access to and freedom to navigate in the Strait of Malacca. Among other considerations, virtually all of Japan's absolutely essential oil is imported, and most of it (from the Persian Gulf) must pass through this narrow and vulnerable passage. The remainder, which comes from Indonesia, passes through almost the same sea lanes en route to Japan. These considerations have drawn considerable new attention in Japan to the nation's essential inability to protect and secure such vital features of Japan's existence.

Yet Japan is simultaneously inhibited, at least constitutionally, from undertaking any national defense role beyond the home islands, and security conscious Japanese have for years questioned how Japan would be able to resolve this forseeable dilemma. Some have toyed with the notion that Japan might find it constitutionally possible to participate in Pacific region security arrangements through a "United Nations" format—for example in connection with the Indochina settlement—but it has not been necessary to confront such ideas in any pragmatic way. The Singapore proposal, on the other hand, addresses a problem that is recognized as real in Japan, and it has the important virtue of allowing Japan to avoid the need for any unilateral initiative.

Similar considerations apply to Australia, Indonesia and Thailand. No one of these states is pleased with the prospect of full American disengagement, from Southeast Asia in particular, yet none knows precisely what can best be substituted for the role so far played by the U.S. Indonesia in particular is attracted to "regional" arrangements, but its leaders are acutely aware that, acting alone, the Southeast Asian states simply do not have the capacity to contribute persuasively to the continuing security problems of the area. The Australians, who do have considerable capabilities, are nevertheless dead set against any role for themselves that would not have the prior approval of neighboring Indonesia. Indeed, Canberra has gone so far as to ask in effect to be invited to join ASEAN, the five nation economic cooperation group established by Indonesia, Malaysia, Singapore, the Philippines and Thailand.

A proposal like Singapore's, which would seek to integrate the interests and policies of Japan, Australia and the U.S. with those of several of the Southeast Asian states, has strong conceptual attractions. Discussion of some such idea as this would at least move the states in the region away from the dead center of immobilism on which all seem to have foundered ever since the Nixon Doctrine was first announced. From the perspective of the United States, it would represent an acceptable and even desirable alternative to the present uncertainties in the region. Yet a joint Pacific region naval agreement is a far cry from the past condition of American dominance of Pacific strategy, and far also from a posture of full American disengagement. It would call, in other words, for a continued and vital American role in the defense of the Asia Pacific rim, and it may be that Americans will not be prepared for that, even as part of a more genuine multilateral effort.

The alternatives, however, seem even more unacceptable to the U.S., for as we noted at the outset of this discussion, the Asian region continues to represent dangerous and unstable conditions. The opportunities for great-power confrontations are present, and in an environment of Sino–Soviet competition in the Pacific, the dilemmas for Japan in particular are liable to grow. The Japan–U.S. alliance, as the following discussions emphasize, will probably continue to be seen as in the best interests of both Tokyo and Washington, but that relationship itself is under stress. It needs a new and expanded basis, for the conditions of Japan and the U.S. (and the Pacific generally) that led to the San Francisco Treaty of 1951 are profoundly different from those of the mid–1970s. Genuine partnership, to make the point one last time, has been absent, and the Singapore proposal—for a Pacific region naval force that would call for cooperation among essentially like-minded states—could provide a basis for strategy far more appropriate to the conditions of the next decade.

NOTES TO CHAPTER FOURTEEN

1. Roger Hilsman, who was assistant secretary of state for East Asian affairs during the Kennedy administration, for example, has written from

the perspective of 1971 that "No one knows what direction China will take in the years ahead" *The Politics of Policy Making in Defense and Foreign Affairs* (New York: Harper & Row, 1971), p. 55.

2. Not long ago the director of the Institute for Strategic Studies, Francois Duchene, characterized this period as "the moment when East Asia is emerging as the new center of great-power confrontation . . . ," in "A New European Defense Community," *Foreign Affairs,* October 1971, p. 68.

3. See *Toward Disengagement in Asia: A Strategy for American Foreign Policy* (Prentice–Hall, 1969).

4. On this point see John L. Gaddis, "The Truman Doctrine," *Foreign Affairs,* January, 1974, p. 392. He notes there that the "actual policies" of the Truman administration (in contrast to some rhetoric) in the period 1947–50 indicate that "the Administration appears to have been seeking a world in which several centers of powers could exist, each exerting a restraining influence upon the other." Insofar as East Asia is concerned, this certainly is the position to which I too have come (see Chapters 4 & 5 in my *Toward Disengagement in Asia*).

5. Nor should it be thought that China came to this posture altogether automatically or inevitably. The strong and "forward" role of the United States during these past twenty years has been a factor of crucial importance in helping the Chinese leadership to conclude that in East Asia it is both necessary and possible to adopt a policy of live and let live.

6. Lee's proposal for a "joint naval task force" came while on a visit to Tokyo in May, 1973, and initially included a "West European" element, by which he no doubt meant Britain. There was an immediate negative Soviet reaction in *Pravda* on May 13, and Japanese officials (Lee met with Tanaka and Defense Agency leaders) appear to have responded that the U.S. probably would not totally withdraw from the region (see *Asia Research Bulletin,* May 1–31, 1973, p. 1831).

Chapter Fifteen

Japan's Security Posture Before and After the Nixon Shocks

Haruhiro Fukui

POSTWAR JAPANESE SECURITY POSTURE

Basic Assumptions

For a little over twenty years since the peace treaty was signed in 1951 in San Francisco and she regained her political sovereignty, Japan has been sometimes praised and sometimes criticized for her apparent reluctance to build a military capability at a pace and to a level "commensurate" with her economic power. Depending on whether one assumed that Japan would stand on one side or on the other in a future military conflict, her rearmament was either commended or condemned. Until a few years ago the governments of the United States and, somewhat less enthusiastically, other "free world" nations welcomed Japan's rearmament and often even prodded her to build up a larger and more efficient force more speedily. On the other hand, the Soviet Union, the People's Republic of China and, somewhat more hesitantly, most governments in Asia and the West Pacific often expressed dismay and misgivings at the prospect of Japan's expanded military and political power and role in the region.

The attitudes of the successive Japanese cabinets seem, however, to have been determined by domestic political factors and pressures rather than by the opinions of the foreign governments and peoples. Of the many domestic factors which contributed to the shaping of Japanese governments' security posture, two seem to have been of special importance. One is the continuous, virtually frozen, divisions of opinion between the major political groups, particularly between the ruling Liberal Democratic Party (LNP) and the four opposition parties. The other was the fragility and instability of the consensus on the issue of national security that obtained among members of the majority.

Much has been said and written about the causes and effects of the perpetual conflicts between the LDP and its supporters on the one hand and the Communists (the JCP), the Socialists (the JSP), the Democratic Socialists (the

143

DSP) and the Clean Government Party (the CGP) on the other.[1] Suffice it here to point out that the latter have remained a numerical minority both among the nation's electorate and elected members of the Diet, but a minority sufficiently large and active to restrain, if not inhibit, government actions of which they disapproved. One of the basic and constant ingredients of the opposition belief system has been a doctrinal and emotional commitment to a form of pacifism born and bred in the cradle of deprivation and destruction during World War II and sanctioned by an explicit provision of the new postwar constitution of Japan.[2] The opposition parties obviously took this commitment quite seriously and were ready to engage in fierce verbal and sometimes physical battles with the LDP, who at times either ignored or challenged their pacifist sensibilities. Generally, however, the LDP preferred to avoid provoking the opposition parties by leaving alone the potentially explosive issue of national security and rearmament.

The LDP and its supporters were considerably less sensitive than the opposition about the constitutional proscription against rearmament or about the popular "nuclear allergy." It is almost exclusively from among the conservative ranks that advocates of Japan's large-scale rearmament and a great-power role in world politics arose. And yet it is a mistake to regard these advocates of remilitarization, especially those who spoke out for nuclear armament, either as typical or representative of the mainstream conservatives. The fact is that the antimilitary pacifist sentiments ran strong among a majority of conservatives both inside and outside the LDP. That is why the successive LDP cabinets consistently refrained from initiating more ambitious military build-up programs and maintained instead a generally low military profile both domestically and internationally.

Underlying the widely shared antipathy of Japanese leaders and masses towards large-scale armament were a series of implicit assumptions about the nature of war, armament, international politics and economy, Japan's status and interests in the world, the level of external threat to Japan's security, the U.S.–Japan alliance, etc. Some of these assumptions were so deeply internalized by so many individuals in postwar Japan that they may be said to have comprised the national credo of the reformed Japanese. Several of these assumptions issued from the deep-running and almost fatalistic sense of Japan's vulnerability under the configuration of power and resource distribution in the postwar world.

Basic to the antimilitary frame of the postwar Japanese mentality were the memories of the last months of World War II, the memories of ubiquitous death, destruction and starvation. The war-renouncing clause of the American-authored 1947 constitution survived the end of the Allied occupation and became an integral part of Japanese political culture in the '50s and '60s largely because the generation of Japanese who were adult members of the society during these decades were those who had lived through the war years and had lost not only their belief but even interest in wars and instruments of war. Their disillusionment with arms and troops as a means by which to achieve national or personal goals was compounded by the emergence of nuclear weapons. Not only were the Japanese the first and so far the only witnesses to and victims of atomic bombs used in combat but they were the most likely potential victims of any future large-scale nuclear warfare. Most Japanese were aware of their singular vulnerability to a nuclear attack, which derived from the physical characteristics of the country and its basic socioeconomic structure and was therefore beyond human control or repair.

Furthermore, throughout the '50s and well into the '60s, the predominant positions of the United States and the Soviet Union in the global balance of military power seemed to be virtually immutable, at least as far as Japan was concerned. The military capability gap, especially relating to nuclear weapons, between the two giants and Japan seemed so infinitely vast that it was patently absurd for the Japanese government ever to contemplate militarily challenging or competing with either of them in a foreseeable future. Considering the extent of her basic military and economic vulnerability, Japan could not realistically challenge even China, especially after the latter had acquired a nuclear capability of her own.

On top of the impracticability of developing a viable independent military force from a purely strategic point of view, political considerations about the likely reactions of the neighboring governments and peoples to Japan's military role further discouraged her leaders from advocating a higher security posture. As I suggested earlier, Japan's rearmament was not welcomed by her Asian and Pacific neighbors. The wariness toward a rearmed Japan, based largely on the memories of the wartime Japanese occupation, acquired a special political significance in postcolonial Asia. If there had ever been some genuine support for a militarily powerful Japan among Asian leaders of the 1930s and the first years of World War II, there was obviously no such sympathy for a remilitarized Japan in the Asia of the '50s and '60s. Many Japanese were aware of this prevailing climate of opinion in Asia and were anxious to dispell their neighbors' fear and misgivings by publicly recanting their prewar militarism and renouncing its revival in postwar Japan.

Another cluster of assumptions was based on a much more optimistic appraisal and projection of Japan's economic capability and growth potential. Largely thanks to American assistance during the occupation, Japan's economy recovered after the end of World War II with a remarkable speed. Ironically, both the general international political conditions generated by the postwar cold war between Washington and Moscow and the special military procurement boom caused by the hot war in Korea contributed to the economic resurrection of the war-weary Japan of the late '40s and early '50s. By the mid–50s not only had her economic production recovered to the peak prewar level but she had been accepted back into the international economic community. During the next fifteen years, the Japanese economy registered phenomenal growth, until she has come to be counted as an economic great power.

Apart from the coincidences of the cold and the hot wars, the post-war economic recovery and development of Japan was made possible by the relatively free access she enjoyed to overseas sources of raw materials and markets. The fortuitous combination of circumstances led many Japanese leaders to believe that Japan would somehow continue indefinitely to enjoy the same degree of access to those raw materials essential for her industry and to markets for her ever growing volumes of products, both far beyond her boundaries. As long as Japan was assured of such access, she was bound to prosper, thought the Japanese leaders, at least in terms of purely material well-being. From the point of view of the Japanese government and people, the pursuit of economic prosperity by the peaceful means of free trade was the most rational and practical way to safeguard and enhance the nation's national interests. Since this could not possibly threaten or offend other nations, Japan would not get involved in the international games of power politics, much less in armed conflicts. It was, therefore, neither desirable nor necessary to build a substantial military capability of her own in anticipation of international complications involving the use or threat of force either against or by Japan herself.

A third group of assumptions related to the evaluation of actual and potential external threats to Japan's security. Generally speaking, most Japanese leaders failed to perceive the kind of imminent threat of aggression or subversion from either of Japan's two major communist neighbors, the Soviet Union and China, which most postwar American leaders from President Truman to President Johnson apparently perceived. During the initial phases of the postwar cold war, Japan was effectively insulated by the protective shield of the American occupation forces from the physical and psychological effects of the global power struggle. After the occupation officially came to an end in 1952, Japan continued to be protected against major external aggression by the presence of resident American troops. The guarantee of protection by the United States was explicitly provided under the terms of the U.S.–Japan Mutual Security Treaty which was signed simultaneously with the peace treaty. Japan has since lived under the American "nuclear umbrella," the presence and efficacy of which have been generally believed by the Japanese government and people, though they have not been actually tested or proven.

The Korean War, which broke out in the middle of 1950, brought the theater of a hot war right next to Japan herself. There were no doubt serious concerns among Japan's political and intellectual circles about the possibility of the nation's direct involvement. The impact of the sense of physical proximity to the theater of fighting contributed to the general acceptance of, or at least acquiescence in, the creation of a small army and the beginning of a rearmament program at General MacArthur's order. The process started then led within a few years to the re-establishment of fully fledged military services euphemistically called the Self Defense Forces (SDF). Important as it was, however, the Korean War did not revive a firm and lasting interest in the problem of national defense and security either among LDP leaders and senior bureaucrats or among the masses of Japanese people. For one thing, the war was, after all, somebody else's—i.e., it was a quarrel between the opposing groups of Koreans, Americans and Chinese. For another, Japan did not really suffer from the war but enormously benefited from it economically. To many Japanese businessmen and workers the war was as much an economic godsend as a tragic military event. It may have produced a temporary state of shock among large numbers of Japanese citizens, but it did not leave on them a lasting fear and hatred of communism, or of the Russians, the Chinese or the North Koreans, as it obviously did on Americans.

The Japanese perception of external threat to their security in fact rapidly diminished after the Korean ceasefire and Stalin's death in 1953. During the following several years, many Japanese were persuaded that the world had entered a new age of reconciliation and peaceful coexistence symbolized by the Bandung spirit. They simply did not believe in the seriousness of communist threat to Japan's survival or prosperity. Hence the massive demonstration of opposition to the revision and extension of the U.S.–Japan Mutual Security Treaty in 1960, which was said to run counter to the spirit of the times.[3] In the '60s the Japanese complacency was somewhat shaken by the intensifying Sino–Soviet dispute, the Chinese Cultural Revolution and, particularly, the war in Vietnam and Indochina. None of these events, however, really convinced the majority of Japanese politicians, bureaucrats or ordinary citizens that Japan herself was directly or imminently threatened. The post–Stalinist Soviet Union somehow did not look as sinister and aggressive as it used to in the late '40s and early '50s, while China simply could not be as unscrupulous or ruthless as Americans were trying to make out. Thanks to the "unique" historical and cultural ties between the Chinese and themselves, so reasoned many Japanese leaders and nonleaders, they naturally knew and understood the true Chinese goals and aspirations much better than Americans and Europeans. Whether the assumption was sound or not, it seems undeniable that even LDP politicians and Foreign Ministry and Defense Agency bureaucrats believed in one or another variation of this logic. In any event, they did not believe that China, communist or otherwise, would attempt to attack or subvert Japan without provocation.

Last but not the least important, the Japanese leaders assumed throughout the '50s and '60s that the potential threat to Japan's security that existed despite all that has been said above could be adequately coped with by the American military presence in and around Japan, including the nuclear umbrella. They were sure that the United States would actually come to Japan's rescue in case of emergency, for an attack on Japan would inevitably involve a direct attack on the American bases and troops in Japan, which would amount to an attack on the United States herself. More generally, they believed that

Washington saw United States security interest in protecting the Far East, particularly Japan, Taiwan and South Korea, from domination by a hostile power, meaning either the Soviet Union or China or both. The belief that the United States was seriously committed to the defense of Japan for her own reasons, apart from whatever altruistic motives she might have had in helping Japan, lay at the root of the Japanese government's security posture during the '50s and '60s.

An even more basic assumption underlying Japan's reliance on the American alliance was, of course, that the United States was and would remain for the foreseeable future the most formidable and, in fact, invulnerable military and economic power. The credibility of the American security guarantee, whether conventional or nuclear, depended in the final analysis on the substantial superiority of military and economic power which the United States was believed to hold over both the Soviet Union and China, not to speak of such lesser communist nations in the region as North Korea and North Vietnam.

Up until 1971 the low profile security posture of Japan was continued with a remarkable degree of consistency, largely because most of the above-mentioned assumptions on which that posture rested remained virtually intact, despite some significant changes in the structure of international and domestic politics. The impact of those "objective" changes on the psychological basis of Japan's security (and foreign policy) posture was deflected and blunted, to an important extent, by the conservative force of government decision-making apparatus.

Decision-making Apparatus

Both in theory and practice, the Japanese Diet is a very powerful organ of the state. It exercises the exclusive power to make laws, approve annual government budget appropriations, ratify international treaties and oversee the actions of the administrative bureaucracy. It does not, however, make all or even most of decisions on the most important domestic and foreign policy issues. A basic impediment to effective and autonomous decision making by the Diet in the formulation of policies has been the perpetual partisan divisions among its members. With a few exceptions, all members of the two houses of the Diet belong to one or another of the five major parties and all, again with rare exceptions, vote strictly along party lines on bills and resolutions both in committee and in plenary sessions. To cross the party lines is to engage in an "antiparty conduct," which is subject to stern disciplinary action according to the rules of each and every party.[4] This insures divisions of opinion and votes on all major bills and resolutions along predictable party lines, and makes it impossible for a Dietwide consensus to form behind a particular policy proposal or program.

Objections and criticisms raised by the opposition parties against LDP-sponsored policy proposals could be overridden by the ruling majority in either house, if there was a consensus among members of the majority party. The fact is, however, that there has never been genuine consensus among them over any major foreign policy issue. Considering the range of the heterogeneous, often mutually incompatible, interests the party represents, it would be surprising if a partywide consensus emerged on any issue that is controversial in the society at large. The sensitivity and vulnerability of a Diet member to pressures from his constituency not only magnifies the schisms among party members representing diverse interest groups but also tends to dampen their will to stand up and speak for a position known to be unpopular with an important segment of their constituencies.

As I pointed out earlier, the majority of Japanese voters refused to believe in an immediate threat from the Russians or the Chinese or in spending a substantially greater amount of money for security and defense purposes than the government was currently spending. Mass media, particularly the press to which Diet members were sensitive, was generally more articulately and, if you like, dogmatically committed to the antimilitary pacifist credo. To advocate a "positive" security policy was no doubt to risk one's popularity rating among the electorate and mass media, a price a prudent politician was naturally reluctant to pay.

Another factor which militated against the growth of promilitary pressures within the LDP was the perennial interfactional strife and rivalries. The factions were, for all practical intents and purposes, subgroups within the parliamentary party nearly as durable and autonomous as the party itself. Since the faction's primary purpose and function was to further and promote its affiliates' chances to win preferred party or government positions and ranks as well as to provide them with campaign funds, interfaction relations were essentially ones of perpetual rivalries, maneuvers and mutual exploitation.[5] The premium was on competition rather than on cooperation, on dissensus rather than on consensus. Disagreements on policy issues easily became entangled with interfactional power struggles and were exploited to embarrass and discredit those who belonged to a rival faction or factions. The presence and actions of the factions thus interfered with and often inhibited initiatives for policy innovations from within the ruling party. They particularly weakened the actual power of the party leadership, potentially the most important source of policy innovation.

There were other reasons why the LDP failed to sponsor more ambitious security programs. One may mention, for example, the singular weakness of the party's policy-making apparatus. The 420 or so party-affiliated members of the Diet, who dominated the entire party organization, were evidently much too busy with other Diet-, party- and constituency-related activities to devote ample time or attention to careful examinations of policy problems. The policy department of the LDP secretariat, run by a non-Diet member staff, had neither the manpower nor the intellectual or material resources that formulation of major domestic or foreign policies would have required. Half a dozen full-time policy researchers, assisted by no more than several dozen staff members, were in charge of the entire range of public policy areas, which is to say every conceivable current issue in the society. They could not possibly supply party-affiliated Diet members with either accurate information or helpful advice, much less present sophisticated policy recommendations to them.

All this led LDP politicians to depend heavily on professional bureaucrats in the various ministries and agencies not only for information and advice but also for actual draft policy statements as well as legislative bills. Hence the well-publicized control of Japanese government policy making by a small group of shrewd and sophisticated senior bureaucrats, virtually all of whom issue from the Law Faculty of Tokyo University[6] It should be noted, however, that the bureaucrats, too, had certain important vulnerabilities. Most importantly, they were, unlike their prewar predecessors, collectively subordinate to Diet members under the postwar constitution. Theirs was formally a role of policy enforcement and implementation, rather than one of policy initiation and formulation. In practice as well as in law, they had to look to the Diet for legislation of laws governing their conduct as well as for budget appropriations supporting not only their agency programs but their personal lives as well. The sense of dependence this legal relationship generates among bureaucrats vis-à-vis politicians was far more real and acute than was usually suspected and obviously affected the bureaucrats' perception of the limits of initiatives they could or should properly take in determining major government policies.

For some strange reason, foreign and security policies were believed to be concerned uniquely with "national" interests and therefore to deserve the special attention of the "people's representatives" in the Diet. At the same time, these policies were assumed, again for strange reasons, to be somehow less technically involved than most domestic social and economic issues and, therefore, more amenable to control and management by politicians with no specialized training rather than by professional bureaucrats. These dubious but widely shared assumptions about the nontechnical nature of defense issues tempted many Diet members to intervene more frequently and vigorously in debates over them than in those relating to, say, industrial relocation, railroad passenger fares, higher education, medical insurance, etc. Politicians' active interest and involvement tended to inhibit bureaucrats' initiatives for policy innovation.

The relative weakness of the Defense Agency among the existing government ministries and agencies, especially vis-à-vis the Foreign Ministry, was another factor contributing to the continuation of the low security policy posture of postwar Japan. As suggested by the fact that it has not yet been elevated to the ministry status, despite the sustained efforts of its friends in the LDP, the Defense Agency has been a weak and generally ineffectual branch of the national government bureaucracy. Its despised status mirrored to some extent the antimilitary public and media opinion. It also reflected, however, the peculiar relationship between security policy and foreign policies in general in postwar Japan.

It is almost a cliché that the postwar Japanese foreign policies revolved around her special relationship with the United States. This was as true for security as for economic relations. Even more importantly, Japanese security policy was not just inseparably related to, but was in fact a function of, the U.S.–Japanese military alliance. This made Japan's security policy an integral part of her foreign policy in general and policy towards the United States in particular. Since recommending and implementing foreign policies was a task properly assigned to the Foreign Ministry, the primary responsibility for drafting security-related policy proposals was also claimed in a rather matter of fact manner by the Foreign Ministry rather than by the Defense Agency. One observer within the fledgling "defense community" once drily said to me that "the Foreign Ministry (made) security policy decisions and the Defense Agency implemented them."[7] This is obviously an oversimplification of a complex process, but it seems undeniable that the major part of bureaucratic input in the formulation of Japan's security posture during the '50s and '60s came from the American Affairs Bureau of the Foreign Ministry, particularly its First North American and Security divisions, rather than from the Defense Agency.[8]

There were several noteworthy characteristics to be mentioned about the way senior Foreign Ministry officials of the '50s and '60s typically approached a security issue. Needless to say, they were those who had lived through and remembered World War II and those unforgetable years just before and after the war. To many of them those years had been a long nightmare which they had no wish to go through again. And the most unfortunate mistake they had made before December 7, 1941 was that they had willfully or inadvertently let the military take over the control of key foreign policy decisions and lead the nation into the head-on collision with the United States. In a sense they were more dogmatically distrustful of the military than the average Japanese citizens and, at the same time, more deeply committed to the policy to maintain and develop, almost at all costs, economic cooperation and military alliance with the United States. American proddings for Japan's higher military (and political) profile drove them to a dilemma which they solved to some extent by supporting the progressive build-up of the SDF under effective civilian (meaning Foreign Ministry) control.

Another characteristic aspect of the Foreign Ministry bureaucrats' approach to security policy issues was what they called the *ankenshugi* (issue by issue approach). This was a variation of the incrementalist approach to decision making, which is fairly common to any bureaucracy. Instead of laying out a long-term plan based on a decision consciously and carefully made at the outset, it assumes that policy decisions are essentially acts of adaptation to historical contingencies and that a policy is nothing but a series of such discrete decisions viewed in a historical retrospective. This was, in practice, if not in principle, the typical style of decision making in the Foreign Ministry, which gave the actions and words of its officials on major policy issues a distinctly ad hoc, muddling through quality. Since each decision was determined largely by the particular circumstances of the moment, rather than by a well-defined vision of the future, the approach tended to be opportunistic and unprincipled. It discouraged interest in and efforts toward formulation of new and systematic policy lines. In the absence of a defined policy goal and a scenario of prospective actions, the status quo became the sole basis and reference point for each discrete decision.

The peculiarly ad hoc style of decision making in the Foreign Ministry may be attributed to a certain extent to the apparent limitation of resources at its disposal. The ministry's personnel officers complain about the shortages of competent staff personnel who occupy decision making positions in the ministry.[9] These are called "staff officers" and recruited through the higher diplomatic service examination held annually for fresh college graduates aspiring to a high-ranking position in the prestigeous ministry. As of 1971, "staff officers" in the Foreign Ministry numbered about 500, or a fifth of the 2,600 or so currently employed by the ministry. Besides the absolute shortage of man-power represented by these figures, the situation was aggravated by the apparent underutilization of the available personnel. Traditionally, the Foreign Ministry has restricted official participation in intraministry policy debates and delibera-tions to "staff officers" alone. Since nearly half of these officials were assigned to embassies and consulates abroad, there were actually not many more than 200 to 250 of them available at any time at the headquarters in Tokyo. It might not have been too bad if all of them could be freely assigned to any specific policy project; there was, however, a rigid rule in the ministry against that kind of flexibility.

In the Foreign Ministry a particular policy issue went automatically to a small team of officials whose composition was more or less predetermined. The team consisted typically of a division head or two at the bottom, a bureau director and a councillor or two at the middle level, and the vice-minister at the top. Sometimes one of the two deputy vice-ministers might be brought in, but the basic decision unit consisted of half a dozen to a dozen officials of the first four ranks. Depending on the country or region of the world the particular problem concerned and its functional substance (such as cultural, economic, political, security, etc.), the director of a particular regional or functional bureau and the head of a particular division within that bureau would form the nucleus of the team, often complemented by a few additional officials of similar ranks from another bureau or bureaus whose jurisdictional interests were involved. This system aggravated the problem of labor shortages by further straining the limited manpower at the upper levels of the ministry hierarchy, especially because issues inevitably fell unevenly between bureaus and divisions and, as a result, some were more overtaxed of their resources than others. The system also exaggerated the influence of senior officials and belittled that of younger ones. As it was mainly among the ranks of junior officials that dissatisfaction with the status quo tended to concentrate, it indirectly helped sustain the conservative tendencies associated with older officials.

As a result of all this, the Japanese security posture during the twenty years, 1951–71, was consistent in its passivity and timidity, as I noted at the outset. The nation's annual military spending actually represented steadily shrinking percentages both of the annual government budgets (12.6 percent in 1955, 8.9 percent in 1960, 8.1 percent in 1965, 7.2 percent in 1970) and of the GNP (1.5 percent in 1955, 0.9 percent in 1960 and 1965, 0.8 percent in 1970), although the absolute value of appropriations under each five year plan was twice as large as that of the preceding one.[10]

More importantly, Japan had no consciously and carefully defined long-term security policy or plan. The Japanese government leaders not only failed to explain to others but did not know themselves what or whom they were building the SDF against, what types and levels of security functions they were supposed to perform in what kinds of situations for what duration, etc. What the Japanese government had during the twenty year period really did not amount to a policy but merely to a posture. It was not until after the Nixon shocks that national security as an issue of policy began seriously to interest Japanese leaders for the first time since 1945.

NIXON SHOCKS AND AFTER

Short-term Effects

Japanese reactions to the two "Nixon shocks" in the summer of 1971 were by no means simple and uniform. For reasons not difficult to understand, reactions to the first "China" shock of July 15, 1971, were much more diverse and complex than those to the second "economic" shock one month later. For one thing, China had been an intensely controversial domestic issue in Japan ever since the time of the San Francisco Peace Treaty. There were clear-cut battle lines drawn between pro-Peking and anti-Peking groups, and the successive LDP cabinets, including Sato's, had been unambiguously identified with the latter. In reply to the opposition's charges of unreasonable and dangerously provocative attitude toward Peking, LDP leaders had been arguing that, first, for historical, political and legal reasons, Japan owed allegiance to Taipei rather than to Peking and, second, to befriend the latter at the former's expense would not only displease Chiang's government but would damage U.S.–Japanese relations. Since the "political and legal" ties between Tokyo and Taipei had issued largely from the peace treaty between the two governments concluded in 1952 under United States pressure, Japan's alleged obligations were essentially an extension or consequence of her obligations to Washington. Apart from some elements of sentimentalism, Japan's refusal to recognize and establish diplomatic relations with Peking had been based on and justified by the argument that the United States did not approve it.

Against this background it should not be difficult to understand why Nixon's July 15 announcement to visit Peking, made without advance warning to the Japanese government, should have deeply hurt and embarrassed Sato and his cabinet. It was as if Sato, his foreign minister, Fukuda, his chief cabinet secretary, Hori, etc. were suddenly delivered as sacrificial lambs to their vengeful domestic enemies by those in Washington who were supposed to be their trusted friends.

In the LDP it was the leaders of the mainstream Sato and Fukuda factions who suffered most directly and deeply from the "shock," while those of the anti-Sato groups, such as Tanaka, Ohira and Miki, not only did not suffer much but even benefited, to varying degrees, from the event.[11] In the bureaucracy it was the staunchly pro-American senior officials of the Foreign Ministry who were badly hurt, while the more independent-minded younger officials in that ministry, and nationalist elements scattered throughout other ministries and agencies, cynically and calmly watched the dismay and panic that overtook the mainstreamers. All were "shocked" by the announcement, which none had anticipated coming at that time and in that manner. Some felt personally hurt by it, while others were surprised but at the same time saw some personal advantage in the event itself or the way it had happened. Depending on where one stood, one reacted either negatively, neutrally or even positively to the shocking event. What mattered really was not so much the event of July 15 itself, but rather its implications for domestic and intraparty politics. In this sense, the China shock was as much an issue between rival Japanese groups as an issue between the two governments of Japan and the United States. Ironically, the customarily most staunchly pro-American groups were hurt most and tended to react most negatively to the American action.

On trade and currency issues, on the other hand, there were no clear-cut partisan or factional splits of opinion. As a result, reactions to the August 15 announcement were far less complicated. Its net effect was, however, a further aggravation of the plight of the pro-American LDP mainstream. Coming as it did on the heel of the China shock, it further eroded what was left of their credibility and authority and added to that of their critics both inside and outside the party.

The blow which the second shock dealt to the LDP mainstream was probably the more serious and lasting. The China shock was caused, after all, largely by an alleged procedural and technical fault in Washington's handling of the matter. Sato and his friends felt that they should have been briefed in advance by the United States government about the preparations under way for Nixon's Peking trip. They were sorry and upset that Washington had not honored its repeated promise to work closely in cooperation with Tokyo in dealing with the China issue, both inside and outside the United Nations.[12]

They could, however, forgive and forget the unhappy experience, if Nixon properly apologized and promised not to repeat the mistake, as he indeed did at San Clemente next January.

The economic shock, on the other hand, was not just a matter of losing or saving a particular Japanese politician's face. It directly concerned Japan's long-term economic interests, which in turn concerned the prospects of continued LDP rule. The LDP's electoral success depended on the sustained economic boom which Japan had enjoyed under LDP rule for nearly two decades. The nation's economic prosperity depended, to an important extent, on her thriving foreign trade, which in turn depended on the favorable exchange rate of Japanese currency and the relatively free access of her products to overseas markets, particularly the United States. The second Nixon shock threatened to destroy these basic conditions for Japan's economic success and, therefore, for the LDP's electoral success. It did not convert the pro-American LDP leaders and senior bureaucrats to overt anti-Americanism, but it certainly shook their confidence and strengthened the positions of the opposition parties and dissenters in the ruling party and the bureaucracy.

Outside the circles of the ruling elites, the two Nixon shocks impressed upon Japan's general public and mass media unacceptable elements of unpredictability and inscrutability of United States foreign policy behavior under the Nixon administration. They immensely helped the image settle in the minds of ordinary Japanese of a secretive, devious, arrogant and obviously anti-Japanese Henry Kissinger, plotting in Washington and in other capitals of the world a new international political order calculated to prejudice Japan's interests. And the negative image of Kissinger and his scheme was generalized into an image of the American government and its official foreign policy line. The change in the Japanese public image of the United States and U.S.–Japanese relations was reflected in the results of several nationwide opinion polls taken before and after the two Nixon shocks.

To give a few examples, a May 1971 *Asahi Shimbun* poll reported that 34 percent of the respondents felt that the U.S.–Japan Mutual Security Treaty was beneficial to Japan as compared with 20 percent who felt that it was not.[13] 25 percent thought U.S.–Japanese relations would improve during the '70s, 26 percent expected not much change one way or the other and 21 percent predicted deterioration. An October 1971 *Yomiuri Shimbun* poll, on the other hand, found 2 percent of the respondents suggesting that the Japanese government positively cooperate in the implementation of President Nixon's economic policy designed to save the dollar, 17 percent that it should cooperate to the extent possible, 22 percent preferring their government taking countermeasures jointly with European nations and 6 percent advocating Japan's simple and unilateral refusal to cooperate with the Nixon government.[14] Even more significantly, only 7 percent chose the United States as the nation Japan should regard as her principal trading partner in the future, as compared with 35 percent who chose China and 17 percent who mentioned Southeast Asia. Thirty-eight percent believed that the United States would *not* really defend Japan in case of emergency, in accordance with the terms of the Mutual Security Treaty, while only 30 percent believed that she would. As many as 32 percent were uncertain and refused to agree with either of the opposite predictions.

The effects of the Nixon shocks on the Japanese public's attitude toward the issue of national security and self-defense seem to have been rather marginal at least in the short run. According to a June 1971 *Mainichi Shimbun* poll, the existing Self Defense Forces were believed to be necessary by 24 percent of the respondents.[15] On the other hand, only 8 percent favored increased military spending, as compared with 38 percent who thought the current level of spending to be adequate, 28 percent who proposed cutting down the current amount and 11 percent who advocated outright abolition of the SDF. In the October *Yomiuri* poll quoted above, those who favored a larger defense capability for Japan remained 10 percent, although 34 percent felt that an increase in military spending would become unavoidable. Forty percent were opposed to an expansion of the SDF and 15 percent were undecided. This seems to indicate that the public attitude had not significantly changed just after the shocks. In the long run, however, there may emerge an attitude somewhat different from the present one. There are, in fact, some indications already that a serious reappraisal of the current posture and the basic assumptions underlying it is under way among some key government officials and intellectuals.

Most Japanese leaders and, presumably, most of the people have believed for more than twenty years that Japan was basically incapable of defending herself against an attack by a great power; that, fortunately, the possibility that one of the great powers would actually mount an attack on Japan was rather slight, at least in the foreseeable future; and that, if that small possibility should materialize, the United States would come to defend Japan according to the terms of the U.S.–Japan Mutual Security Treaty. There was obviously an element of contradiction or at least ambiguity in this line of logic. If Japan was basically indefensible, due to her special geographical and physical characteristics, how could she be defended by the United States? If, on the other hand, the United States was capable of defending Japan, presumably because of her superior military capability, why could not Japan acquire her own military capability, perhaps not comparable to the United States' but as substantial as that part of the United States capability which would be used to defend Japan in case of emergency? If the external threat to Japan's security really did not exist, why should she be protected by the United States? These ambiguities existed in Japan's security posture throughout the postwar years, but now some new problems have been added. The most serious of these was the loss of credibility of the American military guarantee based on the Mutual Security Treaty.

The public opinion poll quoted above indicates the low level of credibility the Japanese public gave to the Mutual Security Treaty and the

American commitments under its terms. Similar skepticism has been voiced by a number of influential LDP politicians and high-ranking bureaucrats I have interviewed during the past several years. As the United States détente with China and the Soviet Union and the withdrawal of her troops from Asia progress under the Nixon Doctrine, the credibility of the American guarantee for Japan's security is bound to decline further. The diminution of the credibility of the Mutual Security Treaty will accelerate and be accelerated by the actual closedown of American military bases in and around Japan. If the United States is not likely to use her troops to defend Japan in case of emergency, why should they be allowed to stay in Japan? As the opposition has been saying all along, the government should ask the United States to close down the bases and call back the troops. But when the bases and troops are gone, the United States would definitely not come to Japan's rescue when she is trouble. The Mutual Security Treaty will have then become even less credible than it is today.

The opposition in Japan to the American military bases has actually intensified for far more complex reasons. For one thing, the rapid spread of urban sprawls has brought large populations to those outlying areas which were once only sparsely populated and where, for that reason, many of the bases of the imperial Japanese army and navy were located. These bases were taken over by the American forces after World War II. A military base in the midst of a densely populated suburb cannot be popular, and cries of "base pollution" are bound to rise.

The recent victories of opposition candidates in gubernatorial and mayoral elections in metropolitan and suburban districts have been another factor. In cities like Yokohama, Tachikawa, Kita Fuji, etc. the antibase campaigns have not only been approved but often led by the mayors elected on joint JCP–JSP tickets. The association and frequent implication of the American bases in Japan with the unpopular war in Indochina has no doubt added to the public hostility toward them. This is particularly true of Kadena and other bases in Okinawa, but those in mainland Japan have also been tainted by the war to varying degrees. In any event, the opposition to the military bases which issues from these diverse motivations and interests and which, in fact, is not directed solely to the American bases but also to those used by the SDF, has considerably increased during the last several years.

Long-term Impact

The long-term impact of the Nixon shocks and, more generally, of the change in United States foreign policy orientation, on Japan's future security posture in general and the SDF in particular is more subtle and harder to assess. As I have already pointed out, the attitude of the general public does not seem to have been immediately and significantly affected. Nor are there any indications of a basic change in the official LDP position in favor of gradual build-up of the conventional (nonnuclear) capability of the SDF but opposed to a substantial acceleration of the pace of the build-up or permitting the acquisition of nuclear weapons by the SDF. I personally believe that the situation is not likely to change within a few years.

It is true that many of the basic assumptions on which Japan's security posture has rested since 1951 have been significantly affected by the recent changes in the general context of international politics and, more specifically, in United States foreign policy and Japan's status in the world economy and politics. As I suggested above, the belief that the United States will actually protect Japan against external aggression at a substantial risk to her own security, because of the U.S.–Japan Mutual Security Treaty, is no longer as widely and firmly held by Japanese leaders and masses. The assumption of Japan's assured access to foreign sources of raw materials and markets has been shaken by the events of the last two years or so, particularly with regard to the import of oil and other energy resources and the export of industrial products. The perception of Japan's economic vulnerability has been dulled to some extent by the sense of affluence and self-confidence generated by the phenomenal growth of the nation's GNP but, at the same time, sharpened by the rapid erosion of the assumption of her free access to overseas resources and markets. These changes naturally cause tensions and anxieties which can potentially generate mass hysteria and the rise of irrational chauvinism. The mass psychology of jingoism thus generated by real and imagined fear and desperation will be susceptible to manipulation by "militarist" politicians and bureaucrats interested in using it as leverage for a drastically accelerated rearmament program.

On the other hand, another very important assumption of the pre-Nixon shock Japanese security posture—the assumption that Japan does not face a serious threat of imminent aggression from outside—has not basically changed. In fact, it has been substantially strengthened by the U.S.–Chinese and U.S.–Soviet détente which the Nixon shocks reflected and advanced. The majority of Japanese leaders and people today feel far more secure from military threat from the communist neighbors than at any time since 1951 and, ironically, vastly more vulnerable to the threat of domestic social and economic ills. High on their minds today are not the possibilities of subversion or infiltration from the continent but the collapse of the system under the weight of the spreading pollution of the environment, the growing congestion of the cities, the visible strains on the transportation facilities, the spiraling costs of living, the rampant speculation in land and important commodities, etc.

The lack of the sense of immediate external threat considerably moderates, if not completely eliminates, the anxieties caused by the declining credibility of the American defense commitments. It is far more likely for the popular frustration and fear caused by the increasing difficulties Japan faces in international trade and economy to generate pressure not for larger armament but rather for better financed and more effective domestic social policies and programs.

Furthermore, it should be remembered that none of the factors inherent in the government decision-making apparatus which militate against policy innovations in the security area have changed or are likely to change in a foreseeable future. The Diet remains deeply and bitterly divided. The LDP is apparently no more capable of making important policies on its own than before the summer of 1971. If anything, the party's control of the Diet is considerably weaker today under Tanaka's leadership than it was under his predecessors. There is a distinct possibility that the LDP may lose its majority position in both houses within a few years. A time of crisis has always been a time of escalated interfactional strife and internecine machination in the LDP, rather than one of genuine and serious policy debates. The Foreign Ministry and Defense Agency bureaucrats have not increased their capabilities to initiate important new policy programs and get them to be accepted by the cabinet and the Diet. In short, the conditions for a basic change in Japan's security posture simply do not seem to exist today any more than they did before the Nixon shocks.

It will be a mistake, however, to conclude that really nothing has changed in the domestic environment of Japan's defense policy decision making as a result of the Nixon shocks. For, to be sure, the erosion of some of the important assumptions of the postwar Japanese security posture which I mentioned has generated some pressure for a change in some areas and at some levels. Public debates on security-related issues, both inside and outside the Diet, are one area in which we can detect a change.

In the Diet opposition members have engaged more vigorously and tenaciously than previously in debates on defense budgets and related matters. These ranged from the relevance of the normalization of diplomatic relation with China to Japan's defense build-up program, the constitutionality of the government decision to equip the SDF with missiles and rockets, the impact of military spending on social welfare programs, distinctions between an offensive and a defensive weapon, etc. The subjects taken up were not new, but the tone of the debates was more serious than during the previous sessions.

Outside the Diet, too, debates on the problem of national security have thrived. For the first time since 1951 current and former government officials deliberately involved themselves in the public debates. For example, the current Defense College president, the former general secretary of the National Defense Council and a former vice-minister of international trade and industry have each written and published a book on the subject of national defense and security.[16] So far, these debates have not led to much more than an escalation of the decades-old verbal battles between the LDP leadership and the opposition parties; between "economists" and "militarists" in the bureaucracy; and between hawks and doves among the general public. It is interesting and significant that no drastic change in the current general posture has been publicly advocated by any representatives or spokesmen of the government or the LDP. Even the Defense College president, who took a position closest to that of the military

among the major protagonists in the debates outside the Diet, explicitly re-
nounced the suggestion that the SDF should or would ever acquire nuclear
weapons.

The change in Japanese perception of and attitude toward the
United States and U.S.–Japanese relations may be more substantial and lasting.
Whatever the ultimate shape of Japan's own security posture which emerges out
of the present uncertainty and ambiguity, it is likely to be less dependent upon
and tied to the military alliance with the United States. In fact, the specific
external conditions which have so far sustained the very special relationship
between the two nations since 1945—the cold war frame of international relations, the undisputed supremacy of United States economic and military power
and, above all, the support of the American public for an active, often interven-
tionist, foreign and security policy of their government—either have disappeared
or are disappearing. Domestic support in Japan for that special relationship is
also rapidly dwindling, to a large extent as a result of the Nixon shocks and the
change in the structure of international politics they reflected.

It is highly unlikely for the LDP, even the left-leaning groups in the
party, to grow as overtly critical of the United States and its foreign policy as
the JCP or the JSP. Strict nonalignment and neutralism, whether armed or
unarmed, is an idea quite alien to the LDP leadership. Nor does the scheme of a
four nation nonaggression pact between the United States, the Soviet Union,
China and Japan, in place of the current bilateral mutual security treaty with the
United States, receive much attention from the top LDP leadership. It seems
nevertheless very likely, if not inevitable, that the center of Japanese politics will
shift toward a position less unambiguously pro-American and more articulately
nationalist and self-assertive. The Nixon shocks probably accelerated the pace of
the shift, but it had been underway long before and irrespective of the events of
the summer of 1971. To an important extent, the change was a function of the
temporal distance from personal involvement in World War II and the Allied
occupation following it. The rising generation of politicians, including those of
the LDP, and bureaucrats, including those in the Foreign Ministry, have no
hang-ups of personal remorse and guilt associated with the war or the sense of
indebtedness and obligation to Americans for help received during the occupation. Whatever faint feelings of guilt and inferiority may have survived among
them into the '60s have now been wiped out clean by their observations of the
recent events in or involving the United States, particularly the war in Indochina.

In the 1969 House of Representatives elections, 48 percent of all
members elected belonged to the "Meiji generation" (born before 1911) and
only 13 percent to the "Showa generation" (born after 1925).[17] Among the
LDP members elected in those elections the percentages were more extreme, 57
percent to 10 percent. In the 1972 House of Representatives elections, however,
the Meiji contingent dropped to 37 percent of all members and 48 percent of
LDP-affiliated members, while the Showa contingent grew to 17 percent and 16

percent respectively. This indicates that the Diet and, to a much greater extent, the LDP parliamentary group are still numerically dominated by the "old generation," but that the balance is shifting in favor of the postwar generation.

In the bureaucracy, too, the Showa generation has been steadily rising in ranks and decision-making power. There are built-in "gerontocratic" tendencies in a system where the rule of seniority is observed as rigidly as in the Japanese government bureaucracy. The system insures, however, periodic changes of those at the top. And twenty-eight years since 1945 those who entered the ministries and agencies after the end of World War II are now beginning to fill the key positions of division heads and assistant division heads. As I suggested earlier, the division head is the lowest-ranking full participant of intraministry policy-making process. In a team formed on a specific policy issue, it is typically the division head, rather than a bureau director or a councillor, who actually investigates the problems involved and drafts policy memos. In day to day operations of the bureaucracy the functions of division heads and assistant division heads are critically important. Their role assumes a particular significance now because of the special generational problems existing between the "wartime" and "postwar" generations of officials, especially in the Foreign Ministry.

Most of the officials currently occupying the bureau director and councillor positions in the Foreign Ministry, just above the ranks of division heads which are already filled by members of the postwar generation, are those who joined the ministry just before or during the war. They were recruited at a time when the best of the nation's youth were drafted into the military services and went to war, when there were no rigorous competitive examinations for diplomatic services as exist today, and when there were no sophisticated training programs for new recruits. In fact, many of these senior officials were not adequately trained in foreign languages nor did they study abroad either while students or during the first years of their professional life after graduation from college, except for military or military-related services in China and Southeast Asia during the war years. Their first "foreign service" training was provided by the Postwar Liaison Offices, which represented the Japanese government to the supreme commander for the Allied Powers (the SCAP) during the Allied occupation, but not to any individual foreign governments. From the point of view of the rising postwar generation, their superiors are therefore terribly inexperienced and clumsy in their dealings with foreign governments and their representatives.[18]

The younger generation in the bureaucracy in general and the Foreign Ministry in particular is impatient with and scornful of the older generation. The latter is often intimidated and reluctant to challenge the "young turks." The current "glut" of bureau director and councillor level personnel tends to slow down the pace of promotions for the disgruntled younger officials and add to their irritations and dissatisfactions, which in turn tend to make them more defiant and intransigent vis-à-vis their superiors not only over personnel matters but also over policy issues.

The growing pressure of the postwar generation in the ruling party and the bureaucracy will inevitably raise the quotient of nationalism and self-assertiveness in Japan's foreign and security policy posture. The trend among the elites will interact with and be reinforced by the rise of nationalism among the masses which has become increasingly evident during the last decade. And nationalism often leads to chauvinism and jingoism. A mass movement for a more active security policy, perhaps instigated and exploited by a segment of conservative politicians and bureaucrats, may well emerge once again to drive the nation toward a military great-power status, "commensurate" with her economic power. Such a movement can be potentially triggered by an external event as well as fermented by domestic pressure. One can think, for example, of abrupt termination of the U.S.–Japanese military alliance based on the Mutual Security Treaty, resulting in a wholesale withdrawal of United States troops, including the Seventh Fleet, from the bases in and around Japan; or the acquisition of nuclear weapons, perhaps small tactical ones, by either South or North Korea; or a serious dispute between Japan and either Taiwan or Korea, involving an issue of national honor or territory; or repeated provocations and humiliations by the nuclear powers, including the United States, etc. For the moment, however, these belong to the realm of possibilities, rather than the realm of probability. And the government and people of Japan are apparently preoccupied now with pressing domestic problems rather than with the question of security and defense against hypothetical external enemies.

In short, my hunch is that, at least for the rest of the present decade, Japan will continue with a security posture much the same as the one she currently pursues. With neither a viable independent defense capability nor a carefully thought out long-term strategic policy, she will continue to drift by instinctive adaptation and piecemeal adjustments. She will thus remain a target of praise on account of her pragmatism and pacifism and, at the same time, of as much condemnation on account of her alleged irresponsibility and insensitivity in the new "multipolar" phase of international politics. The Nixon shocks have thus neither resolved nor clarified the basic problems of Japan's security policy. They have merely accelerated the pace of the nationalist revival which had been under way for two decades.

NOTES TO CHAPTER FIFTEEN

1. See, for example, Robert A. Scalapino and Junnosuke Masumi, *Parties and Politics in Contemporary Japan* (Berkeley: University of California Press, 1962); Nihon Seiji Gakkai, ed., *Nempō Seijigaku 1967: Gendai Nihon no Seitō to Kanryō* (Iwanami Shoten, 1967).

2. See Haruhiro Fukui, "Twenty Years of Revisionism" in *The Constitution of Japan: Its First Twenty Years, 1947–67,* Dan F. Henderson, ed. (Seattle: University of Washington Press, 1968).

3. For a detailed discussion of the anti-Security Treaty campaigns by the opposition groups in 1959–60, see George R. Packard III, *Protest in Tokyo: The Security Treaty Crisis of 1960* (Princeton, N.J.: Princeton University Press, 1966). An exhaustive compilation of information and data relevant to the topic is found in Naikaku-kambō Naikaku Chōsa-shitsu, ed., *Ampo Kaitei Mondai no Kiroku,* December 1961.

4. I discussed this particular problem and its implications for the overall effectiveness of the Diet in "Kokkai no Kinō Kaifuku e no Teigen," *Jiji,* June 1972.

5. I discussed the major functions of the faction in the LDP in *Party in Power: The Japanese Liberal-Democrats and Policy Making* (Berkeley: University of California-Press, 1970), Chapter 5. See also Nathaniel B. Thayer, *How The Conservatives Rule Japan* (Princeton, N.J.: Princeton University Press, 1969), Chapter II.

6. See Shigeo Misawa, "Seisaku Kettei Katei no Gaikan" in Nihon Seiji Gakkai, ed., *Nempō Seijigaku 1967.* For a more general discussion of the higher bureaucrat and his role in Japanese society and politics, see also Akira Kubota, *Higher Civil Servants in Postwar Japan* (Princeton, N.J.: Princeton University Press, 1969).

7. Interview with Makoto Momoi, Head, Planning Office, Defense Academy, October 22, 1971.

8. Interview with Hiroshi Yasuda, Deputy Vice-Minister of Defense, October 26, 1971.

9. This observation is based on interviews with Nagao Hyōdō, Secretary to Foreign Minister Takeo Fukuda, June 29, 1972, and with Nobuo Matsunaga, Head, Personnel Affairs Division, Foreign Ministry, January 28, 1972.

10. Martin Weinstein, *Japan's Postwar Defense Policy, 1947–1968* (New York: Columbia University Press, 1971), Table 2, p. 123.

11. This and following statements are based on interviews with various LDP leaders and Foreign Ministry officials, including Yoshimi Furui, Aiichire Fujiyama, Nobusuke Kishi, Zentaro Kosaka, Masayoshi Ohira and Eisaku Sato among the former, and Shinsaku Hogen, Bunroku Yoshino, Tsutomu Wada, Akitane Kiuchi and Hiroshi Hashimoto among the latter.

12. Interviews with Shigeru Hori, LDP General Secretary, January 24, 1972; Takeo Noda, Chairman, LDP China Committee, February 5, 1972; Nobusuke Kishi, former Prime Minister, March 6, 1973; etc.

13. *Asahi Shimbun,* June 3, 1971.

14. *Yomiuri Shimbun,* October 19, 1971.

15. *Mainichi Shimbun,* June 14, 1971.

16. See Masamichi Inoki, *Kuni wo Mamoru* (Jitsugyo no Nihon Sha, 1972); Osamu Kaihara, *Nihon Retto Shubitai Ron* (Asagumo Shimbun Sha, 1972); Osamu Kaihara et al., "Nihon wa Nani wo Mamoru no ka," *Chūōkōron*, March 1973, pp. 170–184; and Shigeru Sabashi, *Heiwa no Senryaku: Jikken Kokka e no Michi*, 1972.
17. *Mainichi Shimbun*, December 12, 1972.
18. Interviews with Ikuzo Kikuchi, political affairs reporter, *Asahi Shimbun*, April 21, 1972, and with Foreign Ministry officials whose identities cannot be disclosed here.

Chapter Sixteen

New Strategies for the Pacific: Shifting Alliances

Martin E. Weinstein

The purpose of this chapter is to raise the question of whether the U.S.–Japanese alliance will survive the Nixton Doctrine. Firstly, I shall briefly define and interpret current U.S. strategic policy in Asia: and I will explore the alternative, mutually exclusive lines of future development in Asia and toward Japan which are implicit in the Nixon Doctrine.

Second, I will suggest that the development of the doctrine which includes the continuation of the U.S.–Japanese alliance is decidedly advantageous to the U.S., and that the administration, in the long run, probably intends to preserve the alliance, but that for the present it is practicing a policy of calculated ambiguity toward Japan.

And third, I will argue that this policy of calculated ambiguity, combined with the administration's harsh treatment of Japan since 1971, is undermining the alliance in Japan, and that despite the administration's long-range aim of continuing the alliance, its present policy could well lead to the dissolution of the alliance, and to the emergence of a new, but dangerously unstable distribution of power in Asia.

As a first step in defining U.S. strategic policy in Asia, let me state what that policy is not. It is no longer a policy of dispatching American troops to fight on the ground in Southeast Asia in support of Allied or friendly governments. Apart from whether President Thieu will keep his pledge of never again requesting U.S. intervention on the ground, I believe that former Defense Secretary Richardson's statement, that no matter what violations occur in the cease fire we will not reintroduce ground troops into Vietnam, is a firm, fixed element in this administration's policy.

I know that many critics of the Vietnam war make light of this limitation on U.S. involvement, but I do not. I say this because I believe that, ultimately, neither tactical air support, interdiction bombing, the mining of Haiphong, nor even the bombing of Hanoi will determine who governs South

Vietnam or who controls Indochina. That issue is going to be decided by close, small unit combat on the ground. By stating, as it has, that we will not engage in such combat, our government has clearly indicated that if South Vietnam forces, aided by American air, naval and logistical support, cannot hold their own against the North Vietnamese and Vietcong, then we are ready to accept their defeat. This was not American policy ten years ago, five years ago, nor even two or three years ago. It marks a basic change and signifies to me that our government has reduced its military commitment and involvement in Southeast Asia and has begun a process of strategic disengagement, not only in its military presence, but also, and I repeat, in its military commitments, in that part of the world.

This much is clear. What is not clear, is how far and how fast this process of disengagement will continue. Will this disengagement extend to Northeast Asia? Will it, in the course of this decade, lead to the pullback of U.S. naval and air forces to mid-Pacific bases—to staging and support bases in the Hawaiian Islands and forward bases in Guam and the Phillipines. Or, will it lead to the consolidation of the U.S. military position in the Western Pacific based on key naval and air bases in Japan—a position which makes possible the continued U.S. guarantee of Japan's external security.

I suspect that the extent and pace of the disengagement are still uncertain—that while in the long run the administration favors some form of the Western Pacific strategy, for the next few years the policy is to push on with a step by step improvement of relations with the Soviets and the Chinese, and at the same time, to keep under review the possible redeployment of our overseas forces and the redefinition of our overseas commitments so as to reflect the stability and security of the new structure of peace that the administration is hoping to build, in Asia and beyond.

This policy of rapprochement, of flexibility and open options is difficult to take issue with. It responds to domestic political requirements here in the U.S. It suggests that America will no longer be the world's policeman. It implies that a lower percentage of the GNP and the National budget will be allocated to military purposes in the 1970s than in the 1960s. And at the same time, in international strategic terms, it appears to be a careful, realistic policy—a policy which simultaneously takes account of Soviet and Chinese military capabilities and yet manages to scale down American military forces and commitments by employing a rapprochement policy that shrewdly takes advantage of the Sino–Soviet dispute.

This, I believe, is the logic of the Nixon Doctrine, and while it is rational, and to some extent realistic, I do not find it entirely persuasive. As a plan of action, the doctrine is flawed by a disguised yet excessive dependence on the Sino–Soviet dispute, and by excessive optimism over American ability to manipulate that dispute to our future advantage. The administration's foreign policy statements all argue that the doctrine is based on the recognition that we now live in a multipolar, five power world. As a matter of fact, the necessary condition for the workability of the doctrine is not the five power multipolarity; it is, rather, the continuation of the extremely tense but not overtly violent state of Sino–Soviet relations that has persisted since the border clashes in 1969. And yet, it seems apparent to me that the U.S. can hope to exert only a marginal influence on the course of the Sino–Soviet dispute. In brief, the perpetuation of this necessary condition—or to be more concrete, of this specific state of tension in the dispute—is not a matter the U.S. can control, or should count on too heavily.

A second, and to my mind more urgent, flaw flows not only from the logic of the doctrine, but is also a practical flaw, one that grows out of the manner in which the doctrine has been and is being implemented. This flaw centers on our treatment of Japan, and our policy toward the U.S.–Japan alliance.

As I have already suggested, despite its present ambiguity the Nixon doctrine will eventually lead to one of two alternative and mutually exclusive international structures in Northeast Asia. The first of these is a structure in which there is an effective U.S.–Japanese alliance. The second is a structure in which there is not an effective U.S.–Japanese alliance. The first structure is one in which the U.S., together with Japan, maintains a position of virtually unchallengeable naval and air predominance off the coast of Northeast Asia and throughout the Western Pacific. In this structure, the Sino–Soviet dispute is a convenience, perhaps a major convenience, but it is not a necessary condition, for the stability of the structure rests essentially on the predominance of the U.S. and Japan, and not on an equilibrium among the U.S., the Soviet Union, Japan and China.

In the second structure, in which there is no effective U.S.–Japanese alliance and in which the U.S. has withdrawn to the mid-Pacific, the stability of the structure is much less dependable, much less reassuring. For the stability of the second structure depends not only on the assumption that the Sino–Soviet dispute will neither be patched up nor get out of hand; it also depends on the assumption that Japan, without the U.S. alliance, will play a constructive, stabilizing role in this future four power balance—a role that will promote stability and peace in Asia as stability and peace will be perceived and defined in Washington.

Putting it as simply as I can, I believe that it would be an unnecessary and foolishly imprudent risk for the U.S. to give up its alliance with Japan and to move toward a loosely arranged four power balance.

The strongest case for the loose, four power balance is made by Earl Ravenal, most recently in the April 1973 issue of *Foreign Affairs.*[1] As I understand it, Mr. Ravenal's argument is clear and witty, but not entirely serious. At the conclusion of his case for strategic disengagement, Mr. Ravenal acknowledges that his case is an old one, that we tried strategic disengagement in Asia in the

1920s and 1930s but it did not work. According to Ravenal, the main reason it did not work is because, when wars break out abroad and the world seems to be slipping into chaos and violence, disengaged, even pacificist Americans have a disconcerting habit of perceiving strategic interests in odd corners of the world, and in defense of these perceived interests they abandon their proper attitude of disengagement, and dash off to fight wars, sometimes with a crusading zeal that Mr. Ravenal finds distasteful.

The way to make strategic withdrawal work this time around, Mr. Ravenal reasons, is that Americans must cultivate what he calls a sense of equanimity. We must, he claims, learn to tolerate the loss of strategic interests; to live in an increasingly disorderly, violent and unstable world. The logic of Mr. Ravenal's prescription is irrefutable, but its workability depends upon a fundamental and highly unlikely tempermental and philosophical changes in the U.S. Mr. Ravenal's prescription, I believe, is one of the most convincing arguments against the workability of his formula for strategic disengagement and a loose four power balance in Asia.

Mr. Ravenal, however, is not in the government, is not shaping U.S. strategic policy, and I do not believe that the president and Mr. Kissinger are planning to gamble America's future security on our success in cultivating a sense of equanimity. Rather, it appears to me, that our policy is one of calculated ambiguity, an ambiguity that is intended to encourage Soviet and Chinese cooperation with the U.S., and an ambiguity that is also intended to put our allies on notice that they cannot take our support for granted, and by doing so, to strengthen our bargaining position with them over economic and defense issues.

The danger in this intentional ambiguity is that, in the crucial case of Japan, we are carrying it too far and that, as a consequence, we might well end up with a loose four power balance in Asia whether we want it or not.

During the past two years, our government has repeatedly and publicly stated that the U.S.–Japanese alliance is a vital element in U.S. foreign policy. President Nixon made this point in the Shanghai communique in February 1972, at his meeting with Mao Tse-tung and Chou En-lai. He made it again in Hawaii, in late August of 1972, at his last meeting with Prime Minister Tanaka, and this message is repeated consistently in the administration's foreign policy statements. And yet, despite these verbal assurances, American actions toward Japan during the past two years have been provocative and antagonistic.

Let us agree that the 360 yen to the dollar exchange rate was unfair to the U.S. and needed revision. Let us admit that Japanese protectionism needed knocking down. Japan, nevertheless, has been a loyal, dependable ally for more than twenty years. It is not the only source, nor even the major source of America's economic difficulties. Japan did not deserve to be made the scapegoat for these difficulties. The antagonistic, adversary approach that our government has been taking on economic issues has raised and still raises grave doubts among Japan's financial and industrial leaders about American basic long-term intentions—doubts that extend to the reliability of the U.S. as an ally, doubts that continue to feed on President Nixon's public threat, in the fall of 1971, to settle the textile dispute by invoking the Trading With the Enemy Act against Japan. Our government has conveniently forgotten that embarrassment. Among Japanese business leaders, however, who have been a principal source of support for the alliance, it still gnaws and rankles. And our treatment of economic issues since 1971 has done nothing to make them forget that incident.

Even more to the point, our government's secret, unilateral approach to China in the spring of 1971 struck at the very heart of the alliance—the sense of mutual trust—and it struck at the single most important source of Japanese support for the alliance, the foreign policy bureaucracy. Although Mr. Tanaka became Prime Minister as a consequence of that shock, and benefited politically by his own visit to Peking last fall, resentment against the U.S., and a sense of betrayal, runs strong among bureaucrats and conservative political leaders, and it runs far beyond former Prime Minister Sato and his heir apparent, Mr. Fukuda.

In short, while I can accept the logic of an intentionally ambiguous Asian policy, I believe that our ambiguity toward Japan has been producing more than the desired therapeutic unease. Among many influential leading conservatives, this ambiguity has assumed the appearance of an ominous, calculated deceit.

What, they want to know, are the objectives of American rapprochment with China? Why did it have to begin so secretly, and why is it carried on unilaterally? Why does the U.S. accept China's nuclear weapons, while it urges Japan to ratify the Nonproliferation Treaty, and simultaneously forces Japan to up-value its currency 33 percent in the space of eighteen months? Is U.S. policy aimed at building a détente with China while reducing Japan to a permanent military and economic dependency—all in the name of rapprochment and free trade?

It seems to me that these questions, and the doubts that they feed on, have already done great damage to the U.S.–Japanese alliance. I do not think that the alliance can survive another two or three years of the kind of treatment we have been giving it since 1971. If we go on as we are, the damage to the alliance will become irreparable.

The prescription for preserving the alliance is simple and obvious. First, the U.S. should coordinate its China policy with Japan. The Japanese have wanted to do this all along, but we have not been willing to. Second, we must stop making Japan the scapegoat of our economic problems. This does not mean that we ignore our economic differences, or that we will be able to settle them quickly. It means that we should take the same approach toward Japan that we are taking, for instance, toward the West Germans, or toward Western Europe as a whole—that we continue to press and bargain for a world of expanding trade and stable monetary arrangements, without singling out Japan as a special culprit.

In conclusion, let me address myself to one last question: Is the administration likely to make the policy alterations necessary to preserve the U.S.–Japanese alliance? My answer is no, they are not likely to do so. The main reason is that at the present time they do not appreciate the damage they have wreaked and are continuing to wreak in Japan. Conservative control in Japan, and continued adherence to the U.S. alliance, are taken for granted—in my opinion mistakenly so. The conservative coalition which has governed Japan since the 1950s, and its continued support of the U.S. alliance, are believed to be almost infinitely resilient. Underlying this belief is the assumption that no matter how badly we treat Japan on the China question, or on economic issues, they have no long-term rational alternative to continued trade and security dependence on the U.S., that squirm and squeal as they may, they will stick with the alliance.

The key term here is rational alternative. For if we continue to treat the Japanese as we have these past few years, they may not limit their foreign policy to what we perceive as rational alternatives.

In concluding, I am not predicting either the unavoidable dissolution of the U.S.–Japanese alliance, nor am I predicting the inevitability of disaster if the alliance is terminated. I am arguing, rather, that we are safer with the alliance than without it and that, therefore, it is imprudent to continue on our present course of action toward Japan, which places the alliance in great jeopardy.

NOTES TO CHAPTER SIXTEEN

1. Earl C. Ravenal, "The Case for Strategic Disengagement," *Foreign Affairs,* April 1973, pp. 505–522.

Chapter Seventeen

Comments

Angus M. Fraser

Much of what is in the chapters by Fukui and Weinstein suggests that new stresses and changing international relations have upset the Japanese–American understanding that has been built up over the years since 1945. There is some consensus that serious damage has been done to this fabric, but that it is not beyond repair. My task is to deal with the effect that present and prospective conditions might have on future United States strategy in Asia.

Dr. Weinstein sees the Nixon Doctrine as connected with much of the problem. He also believes that ground forces are a primary element in the resolution of conflict in Asia. I agree with the first premise, but I have some reservation about American ground forces in the second. I ask first that we remember the circumstances accompanying the original enunciation of the Nixon Doctrine. It was made at a plane-side press conference on Guam in July of 1969. We must recall that at this point President Nixon had been in office less than six months and he had promised to get the United States out of Vietnam, where we then had some half million men. It was, in part, a message to his domestic constituency—"help me get out of this and I promise we will never get into such a mess again." To allies and others interested in United States security policies and doctrines, he was saying, "we will continue interest and support in your security, but you will have to contribute more, particularly *more of the manpower.*"

Perhaps the best illustration of the meaning of the doctrine may be found in the Republic of Korea. When a massive draw-down of United States troops was first suggested, there was a storm of protest. This was accompanied by a demand for a $5 billion, five year force improvement program. Hard bargaining produced solution. United States troop strength was reduced from just over 60,000 to 43,000, with further withdrawal left as an open question. A wing of USAF F–4 aircraft was assigned a home station in Korea. Finally, the military assistance five year program was set at $1.5 billion.

There are other demonstrations of the American reality, such as substantial diversion of resources provided for equipping and training Cambodian forces. Taiwan, never directly dependent on the massive presence of United States combat troops, also has moved more and more to direct purchase of military hardware and away from grant aid. Other Asian allies have continued to receive assistance and—as far as one can tell—there were no significant reductions in the cost or progress of Vietnamization.

Over the long haul a massive reduction in actual United States presence in Asia and the West Pacific is entirely possible. One of the bars to hasty action is the simple cost of moving. It has been estimated that the retraction of United States present Asian facilities to mid-Pacific would cost something in the neighborhood of $3 billion and the result would be only an increase in travel time to operating areas or sites and the reduction of physical presence. This latter is a factor given varying weight by different interests, but the question of credibility and presence has some importance. There is, of course, a demonstrable set of trade-offs between mobility and presence, but there does seem to be some valid argument for the need of an old-fashioned "trip wire" in the form of exposed American troops. The future does not look easy, but one must think that American strategic and foreign policy thought will continue to reflect adequate awareness of the need for presence and support in Asia. It might be proved that the loss of Japanese bases would make life terribly difficult for the Seventh Fleet, but it is equally true that this would come about only if the Security Treaty were denounced. In this case, a whole new set of considerations would enter. In any case, I cannot see evidence that the United States would abandon its commitment to Asian security, however painful the change to new arrangements might prove to be.

Dr. Fukui gives a clear picture of the domestic situation in Japan, and most particularly of the responses to the so-called "Nixon shocks" by the leaders in Tokyo. The question of "neglect" seems to figure large in Japanese thinking. There seems to be some evidence that Washington does indeed take too much for granted. It has not been unobserved that Dr. Kissinger's staff did not include a specialist in Japanese affairs—a painful contrast with the People's Republic of China or Soviet Union.

Japan sees that there may arise the need to "float" in security matters, avoiding exclusive arrangements as much as possible. The Nixon moves toward better relations with both the People's Republic of China and the Soviet Union have forced some rethinking. All in all, however, Dr. Fukui describes a people who have a passive and conservative stance, a real sense of vulnerability, a distrust of war and a resigned feeling that Japan cannot effectively be defended in modern war. Despite her mixture of feelings and concern over a radically changed situation, the Japanese have not yet made an organized transfer of their internal feelings into programs of action. They are still in the debating phase and it may take as long as twelve years to produce decisive change. This change,

Dr. Fukui says, may include a perceived need for stronger and more independent military forces. Twelve years is a notoriously long period for prediction, particularly in matters as complex and serious as major shifts in military posture. We can only hope that both parties will use the time immediately before us to reconcile differences and find a way of continuing without the introduction of a heavily armed and apprehensive Japan into the Asian equation. Meantime, the United States faces the complex problem arising from the need to reduce costs and maintain commitments and guarantees, while attempting to persuade both allies and foes that the problems of security may be solved by new arrangements and agreements. The total "mix" of elements in the United States strategy is thus being altered, but the role of explicit military force will not be completely eliminated. Future relations with Asian allies will invoke a continuous—and sometimes tense—debate over the adequacy of United States support and protection. I see no evidence that the sort of withdrawal described by Ravenal in the April 1973 *Foreign Affairs* is in any way likely to come about. American changes are those of style rather than of major philosophies.

Notes on Contributors

(Contributors to this volume of essays do not necessarily present the views of the institutions with which they are currently associated.)

Robert W. Barnett—Vice-President, Asia Society. Studied at University of North Carolina and Oxford University, Yale University; Service Far Eastern Affairs, U.S. Department of State. Author of *Economic Shanghai: Hostage to Politics,* (New York: Institute of Pacific Relations, 1943.)

H. Edward English—Director, School of International Affairs, Carleton University. Studied at University of British Columbia; University of California, Berkeley. Author of *Industrial Structure and Canada's International Competitive Position; Transatlantic Economic Community: Canadian Perspectives,* (Toronto: Private Planning Association 1968); *The Impact of Trade Liberalization,* Toronto; Private Planning Association, 1968.

Richard A. Ericson, Jr.—U.S. Department of State. Bureau of East Asian and Pacific Affairs. Studied at Georgetown University, Foreign Service Institute. Service in Japan, Korea, U.K., Australia; Chief, Japan–Korea Bureau, Office for Research and Analysis for Asia, Washington; Foreign Affairs Officer; National War College; Country Director for Japan.

Angus M. Fraser—Colonel, U.S. Marine Corps (Ret.). Served as Senior Marine Advisor, Republic of China, Taiwan. Consultant, Smithsonian Institute, and Historical Evaluation and Research Organization; Staff member Institute for Defense Analysis. Author of *The People's Liberation Army: Communist China's Armed Forces* (New York: Crane, Russak 1973) Strategy Papers No. 19.

Haruhiro Fukui—University of California, Santa Barbara; and Brookings Institution. Studied at Tokyo University, Australian National University. Author of *Party in Power: The Japanese Liberal–Democrats and Policy Making* (Berkeley: University of California Press, 1970); and "Twenty Years of Revisionism" in *The Constitution of Japan,* (Seattle: University of Washington Press, 1968) Dan F. Henderson, ed.

Bernard K. Gordon—University of New Hampshire. Studied at University of Chicago, New York University; visiting professor, American University, Johns Hopkins University, University of Singapore. Author of *Toward Disengagement in Asia* (Englewood Cliffs, N.J.: Prentice–Hall 1969); *Dimensions of Conflict in Southeast Asia* (Englewood Cliffs N.J.: Prentice–Hall, 1966); *New Zealand Becomes a Pacific Power* (Chicago University of Chicago Press, 1962); articles in *Current History, Asian Survey, ORBIS, Solidarity, Pacific Affairs, World Politics, Bulletin of Atomic Scientists.*

Carl Jayarajah—International Bank for Reconstruction and Development. Studied in Ceylon (Sri Lanka) and at London University. Service as Deputy Director of Research in the Central Bank of Ceylon, and as economist in The South Asia Department of IBRD.

Akira Iriye—University of Chicago. Has written extensively on Japanese military expansion, Japanese cosmopolitanism and other topics on Japan. Author of *Across the Pacific: an Inner History of American–East Asian Relations* (New York: Harcourt, Brace and World 1967); *After Imperialism* (Cambridge, Mass.: Harvard University Press, 1965); *Pacific Estrangement: Japanese and American Expansion 1897–1911* (Cambridge, Mass.: Harvard University Press, 1972).

Allen B. Linden—University of New Hampshire. Studied at Wayne State University and Columbia University. Columbia Traveling Fellowship and Ford Foundation Fellowship for research Taiwan and Hong Kong. Author of "Politics and Education in Nationalist China," *Journal of Asian Studies,* August, 1968.

Frank D. McCann—University of New Hampshire. Studied at Niagra University, Kent State University, Indiana University, Pontificia Universidade Catolica de Rio de Janeiro. Author of *The Brazilian–American Alliance 1937–45* (Princeton, New Jersey: Princeton University Press, 1974); articles in *Historia, Inter-American Economic Affairs, Foro Internacional, The Americas, American Historical Review, Perspective.*

Louis C. Morton–Dartmouth College. Studied at New York University, Duke University; visiting lecturer, United States Air Force Academy, Rice University, University of California, San Diego. Rockefeller Public Service Award. Author of *The Fall of the Philippines* (Washington, D.C.: Department of the Army 1953); *War in the Pacific: Strategy and Command* (Washington, D.C.: Department of the Army, 1962); *Theory and Practice in American Politics;* general editor., *Wars and Military Institutions of the United States,* 17 vols. Washington, D.C. Department of the Army, 1968.

Kenneth J. Rothwell–University of New Hampshire. Studied at University of Western Australia, Stockholm University, Harvard University; visiting professor, Institute of Social Studies. Author of *Administrative Issues in Developing Economies* (Lexington: D.C. Heath 1972); co-author *Theoretical Issues in International Economics* (Boston: Houghton Mifflin 1967); editor, *New England–Japan Trade and Exchange Potentials* (Durham, N.H.: New England Center, 1974); articles in *Public Finance, Indian Economic Journal, Kyhlos.*

Masao Sawaki–Consul General of Japan, New York. Studied at Faculty of Law, University of Tokyo. Service in Brazil, Italy, United States; Economic Cooperation Division, Economic Affairs, Tokyo; Counsellor of Economic Cooperation Bureau, Tokyo; Minister of Japanese Embassy, Washington; Ambassador of Japan to the Philippines.

Donald R. Sherk–Simmons College. Studied at University of Iowa, Australian National University. Economic Consultant, Asian Development Bank, Philippines. Author of *The U.S. and the Pacific Trade Basin* (Federal Reserve Bank of San Francisco, 1970.); articles in *American Economic Review.*

Eugene P. Trani–Southern Illinois University and Woodrow Wilson International Center. Studied at University of Notre Dame, Indiana University. Author of *The Treaty of Portsmouth* (Lexington: University of Kentucky Press, 1969); articles in *Review of Politics.*

Martin E. Weinstein–University of Illinois and Brookings Institute. Studied at University of Southern California, Columbia University. Author of *Japan's Postwar Defense Policy* (New York: Columbia University Press, 1971); *Japan: the Risen Sun* (New York: Foreign Policy Association, 1970); articles in *Interpreter, Reporter Magazine, Pacific Affairs, Foreign Policy Association, Current History.*

About the Editors

Bernard K. Gordon is a political scientist who has specialized in foreign policy strategic issues in East Asia. He has a Ph.D. from the University of Chicago and currently teaches at the University of New Hampshire. He is the author of *Toward Disengagement in Asia* (1969); *The Dimensions of Conflict in South East Asia* (1966) and *New Zealand becomes a Pacific Power* (1960).

Kenneth J. Rothwell, an Australian economist with special interests in international economics and development, has served on several United Nations missions on economic and administrative problems. He earned a Ph.D. from Harvard University and is currently on research leave from the University of New Hampshire. He is the author of *Administrative Issues in Developing Economies* (1972) and *Theoretical Issues in International Economics* (1967) as well as several studies on commercial and educational exchanges with Japan.